AMITAVA NAG is an independent film critic based in Kolkata, and editor of *Silhouette* (www.silhouettemagazine.com). His most recent books on cinema are *Murmurs: Silent Steals with Soumitra Chatterjee*, *16 Frames* and *Smriti Satta o Cinema*. His earlier writings include the acclaimed books *Satyajit Ray's Heroes and Heroines* and *Beyond Apu: 20 Favourite Film Roles of Soumitra Chatterjee*.

Amitava also writes poetry and short fiction in Bengali and English. His poetry collection *Forever Meera* and translation anthology of Soumitra Chatterjee's English poems titled *Walking Through the Mist* were published in 2020. He can be reached at www.amitavanag.net.

সৌমিত্র চট্টোপাধ্যায়

ডব্লিউ থ্রি টি সি - নাইন, ফেজ সিক্স
গল্ফ গ্রিন আর্বান কমপ্লেক্স
কোলকাতা – ৭০০০৯৫
দুরভাষ: ২৪৭৩ – ৭৮০৪
মোবাইল: ৯৮৩১১ ৫০০৩১

Tapan Sinha is an important filmmaker in my life. I have mentioned quite a few times that he is the one who actually taught me some of the basics of acting. I have acted in his films in two phases - the first one in the early '60s with 2 films - *Jhinder Bandi* and *Kshudhita Pashan*. I returned with *Atanka, Antardhan* and *Wheel Chair* among others in the '80s and '90s.

Unfortunately, may be due to lack of restoration or so, Tapan-Da's films don't get the necessary mention they should have received. This book is the first on him in English and I sincerely feel this is a much needed one.

I am glad that Amitava has taken up this task and written on him. I hope the book will be helpful for future generations to approach Tapan-Da's work.

I wish Amitava and the book all the success.

Soumitra Chatterjee

28.11.2018

## Praise for Tapan Sinha

"Tapan Sinha had the expertise and vision of a great film-maker. The subject matter of most of his films was contemporary and relevant. You learn a lot and feel good after watching his films. When I think of Tapan Sinha, I think very fondly of a good human being who led an unobtrusive, down-to-earth life and carried on making meaningful films for a long time."

—Sharmila Tagore, actor

"Before working with him, I watched *Sagina* and *Aadmi Aur Aurat*. I was fascinated by *Aadmi Aur Aurat* ... Tapan Sinha was open to listening to actors and providing them with suggestions. He was more in the classic mould. His film-making, shot-taking and his expectations from actors were different from that of Goutam Ghosh or Mrinal Sen. Anyone who has ever worked with him has always spoken warmly about him."

—Shabana Azmi, actor

"Working with Tapan Sinha was a many-splendoured experience because he himself was a man of excellent literary calibre. He picked up subjects that were stimulating and challenging and was so meticulous in drawing out work from each one of his artistes."

—Dilip Kumar, actor

"In 1957, when Tapan Sinha was making Rabindranath Tagore's *Kabuliwala*, I had a chance to work with him as the music director of his film. He was a very sweet-natured person and a wonderful humanitarian ... I always found something valuable to take away from his films. All of them touched my heart. To me, Tapan Sinha was one of the best directors of India."

—Pandit Ravi Shankar, musician

"Tapan Sinha was a true lover of art, truth and beauty, the finesse and depth of which have been successfully portrayed in his work. He is a maestro in the world of cinema."

—Amitabh Bachchan, actor

"Tapan Sinha was an extraordinary person who possessed a strong sense of humanity, love for the people, the capacity and courage to fight for good cinema and voice his opinions ... In his cinema, the camerawork is exquisite because he excelled at his craft. He was a complete film-maker who could traverse the different departments of film-making with poise and ease."

—Buddhadeb Dasgupta, film-maker

"Tapan Sinha was a sensitive film-maker and also a thorough gentleman. He was completely open to ideas and suggestions, and encouraged actors to share them with him. Extremely patient with his actors, this stalwart of Indian cinema provided actors with the necessary time and space to deliver stellar performances."

—Pankaj Kapur, actor

"The best part of Tapan Sinha as a director was the fact that he was never domineering. In whatever he did, he chose to remain understated. That is why I call him an absolute maestro ... He rested his faith on an actor's inherent sensibilities while portraying a character. Being a superb technician himself, he had clarity of thought about what he needed in a scene and the skill to extract the required performances from his cast and crew."

—Amol Palekar, actor

"Tapan Sinha was a man of integrity, unwavering zest for life, complete commitment to his work and genuine affection for all those whose lives he touched."

—Nandita Das, actor

"Tapan Sinha had a fair knowledge about all aspects of film-making and an excellent understanding of music as well. He was a good singer and a fantastic flute player. This helped him to compose music for his films, which is a unique aspect of his cinema. He always kept in mind what the audience would like to watch. He felt, in a sense, accountable to them."

—Madhabi Mukhopadhyay, actor

"Tapan Sinha was a technician himself and that made him a complete film-maker. No other director has made films with so many varied themes and styles ... Every film-maker's contribution needs to be analysed in the context of their time. Tapan Sinha made classical films, comedies, children's films, satire and socially relevant films. He responded eloquently to his time through them."

—Goutam Ghose, film-maker

"It is my bad luck that I worked only in one Tapan Sinha film (*Didi*). He was such a gentle soul and a very sensitive film-maker. He was clear in his mind as to what he wanted in his films. He had an intricate knowledge of cinema and other aspects of art as well."

—Deepti Naval, actor

"It's amazing how Tapan Sinha slowly and calmly moved on from one film to the next. It was as if he had the obvious claim to the keys of the door to unlock the subjects of his films. He would then roam around that house of subjects unobtrusively, moving from one room to the next ... When he worked on a subject he enjoyed it to the fullest and passed on the same enjoyment to his audience as well."

—Rituparno Ghosh, film-maker

"I was extremely fortunate to work with Tapan Sinha though it was for a limited period ... He was a director who was in the same league as Bimal Roy and Manik-da (Satyajit Ray)."

—Shatrughan Sinha, actor

"Tapan Sinha started off within typical mainstream cinema because he believed in making the audience happy and making good the producer's money. Otherwise, making the next film would have become difficult. But his dedication to serious cinema made him experiment constantly in his films ... From a very modest beginning as a commercial film-maker he grew into a serious director. I have not seen this happen to any other film-maker."

—Soumitra Chatterjee, actor

# THE CINEMA OF TAPAN SINHA

## AN INTRODUCTION

AMITAVA NAG

Om Books International

First published in 2021 by

**Om Books International**

**Corporate & Editorial Office**
A-12, Sector 64, Noida 201 301
Uttar Pradesh, India
Phone: +91 120 477 4100
Email: editorial@ombooks.com
Website: www.ombooksinternational.com

**Sales Office**
107, Ansari Road, Darya Ganj,
New Delhi 110 002, India
Phone: +91 11 4000 9000
Fax: +91 11 2327 8091
Email: sales@ombooks.com
Website: www.ombooks.com



ISBN: 978-93-85252-86-0

Printed in India

10 9 8 7 6 5 4 3 2 1

# Contents

# Introduction

Like with most young middle-class boys growing up in the late seventies and early eighties, cinema exerted its disarming charm on me. The larger-than-life projections on huge screens in dark cinema halls left an indelible impression, which will never be matched by the experience of watching films on digital devices like laptops, mobile telephones or modern high-definition TVs. I was brought up in an academic environment with no television at home, and cinema was a restricted entertainment for both me and my sister. Among the few films we were allowed to watch at the cinema hall at an early age was one with a white elephant named Airavat in it. We were familiar with Airavat, the mythological white elephant who is said to have carried Indra, King of the Gods, on his back. We were fascinated by the stories about Airavat, his conquests and stature as the king of all elephants. To our surprise, the Airavat in the film was a far cry from that mythological creature. Nonetheless, we loved him immensely and *Safed Haathi* (The White Elephant, 1978) remained my favourite film for a long time.

Sibu, the film's protagonist who must have been the same age as us at that time, became our role model. *Safed Haathi* is the *desi* version of *The Jungle Book*, which predated the Hollywood film's relevance in the lives of Indian children. As it often happens with young minds, we were not bothered about who the director of the film was. For us, the only important thing was our love for Sibu, the hero, and Airavat, the white elephant. As I grew older and started viewing films from a more serious angle, Tapan Sinha and Satyajit Ray became my favourite film-makers for directing films for adults as well as children and teenagers. Later on, with exposure to the films of other stalwarts, particularly that of the maverick Ritwik Ghatak as well as works of world cinema, my vision enlarged and deepened. Yet, the space Tapan occupied has never shrunk—not because of my childhood weakness for *Safed Haathi*, but due to the many excellent films he made during his five-decade-long career.

In 2014, independent art curator and archivist Sounak Chacraverti organised a three-day-long poster-cum-photograph exhibition on Tapan in Kolkata. Titled *Aponjon*, the exhibition celebrated the 90th birth anniversary of the legendary film-maker. Chacraverti had curated a similar exhibition, but on a bigger scale, in 2008 in Kolkata and at the Film and Television Institute of India (FTII), Pune. I was fortunate to attend the inauguration of the 2014 exhibition, which was marked by the reminiscences of actors, producers of Sinha's films and a note of appreciation from Bollywood superstar Amitabh Bachchan, which read: "Tapan Sinha is a true lover of art, truth and beauty, the finesse and depth of which have been successfully portrayed in his work. He is a maestro in the world of cinema."[1]

Chacraverti later approached me with the idea of bringing out an anthology of articles on Tapan's films, which he wished to edit. He requested me to write a chapter in it.

That project did not see the light of day, but the thought of writing extensively on Tapan started brewing in my mind. I had written tributes and remembrances after his demise in 2009. As with most Bengali film personalities (apart from the stalwarts, Satyajit Ray and Mrinal Sen), there is no proper collection of writings in English on Tapan. I have always been keen to write books in English on personalities of Bengali cinema, hoping that they will become archival material on these greats who are often pushed aside as 'regional'. I wrote my book, *Beyond Apu: 20 Favourite Film Roles of Soumitra Chatterjee,* in 2016, with the same hope.

Siddhartha Kumar Ghosh, Tapan's nephew, says: "Tapan Sinha remained a private, media-shy person throughout his life. He never liked to reflect on himself or his family. That is why very little is known about him."[2]

Tapan's son, Anindya Sinha, related an incident to me once. This revolved around Tapan's response after he had an accident during the shooting of *Aaj Ka Robinhood* (Today's Robinhood, 1987): "At that time, I was staying in a hostel. As was common practice then, my room-mates and I used to share a lot of things including our clothes. When I came to know of Baba's accident, I rushed to Calcutta in a hurry. I was wearing a friend's shirt. Baba was in a lot of pain when I visited him. Even then, he asked me whose shirt I was wearing. He could make out that it was not mine. The next day, when he was feeling better, he told me that I should buy a new shirt and gift it to my friend. He was very particular about not taking advantage of people or accepting undue favours from them. He always advised us to do the same." This reveals an important aspect of Tapan's persona—that of a highly sensitive person with an immense sense of dignity and pride. This could be why there is such a dearth of written material on him. Troubled by this lack, I felt compelled to write a book on the quiet master of cinema.

Most of Tapan's early cinematic masterpieces are based on some of the greatest works of Bengali literature. Along with the strong literary content, which forms the backbone of his scripts, the highlight of most of Tapan's films is the music—playback as well as the background scores. He wrote a number of songs for several of his films even though he would shy away from displaying his name as a lyricist on the title cards along with the greats like Rabindranath Tagore, Dwijendralal Ray, etc. Not even Satyajit Ray, who also composed the music for most of his own films, has written songs for so many films. Tapan was prolific in terms of producing songs and background scores, and his creative process had a natural musical rhythm, which is evident in the flow of his films. They bear traditional literary traits and yet, in his shot composition and editing style, the free-flowing tempo of musical cadence is emphasised.

Tapan was the bridge between arthouse and commercial cinema, the rarest of rare breed during his time. Unfortunately, this bridge no longer exists in Indian cinema. Tapan was a unique example of a director whose films garnered awards at national and international film festivals and also became big box-office successes. The commercial success of his films came from his skilled handling of subjects and the excellence of his craft and not because of the presence of bankable stars. Some of his contemporaries (even in the Hindi film industry), such as Bimal Roy and Hrishikesh Mukherjee who tried to follow a similar path of entertainment and art, almost always cast the biggest stars of the day in their films. In stark contrast, Tapan never once cast the golden on-screen couple of Bengali cinema, Uttam

Kumar and Suchitra Sen, who ruled the roost for three decades from the fifties till 1980, together in any of his films.

Out of all of Tapan's films, five are etched on my mind because of their staggering range—*Kabuliwala, Jhinder Bandi, Jotugriha, Sagina Mahato* and *Ek Doctor Ki Maut*. Tapan's *Kabuliwala* was faithful to the original Tagore story even though he added a number of subplots which enriched the main narrative. In spite of the extremely theatrical makeup of Chhabi Biswas who played Rahmat, the Afghan trader, the film is a sensitive rendition of love and longing. Biswas's histrionics and Tinku Tagore's effortless innocence as Mini captivates the audience even today. The on-screen bond between Rahmat and Mini continues to remain unparalleled on the Indian screen and it cemented Tapan's place as an excellent director of actors. In mostly all his subsequent films, the content varied significantly, but acting remained a highpoint of his craft.

*Jhinder Bandi*, the successful 'Indianised' adaptation of Anthony Hope's *The Prisoner of Zenda*, is one of the oldest Bengali films to showcase drama and suspense in a way very few films of the time achieved. For the first time, it pitted two of Bengal's greatest actors against each other. Uttam Kumar and Soumitra Chatterjee never looked so good together in any other film. This was the first time that Soumitra was cast as a villain, a casting coup of sorts considering the fact that with his aristocratic looks and refined personality, he used to play characters who were derived mostly from Tagore stories. Most importantly, in spite of Soumitra's success in the Ray films that preceded *Jhinder Bandi*, this was the first time the audience actually took notice of the young actor, who was hardly three years old in the trade and had taken on the biggest superstar of Bengali cinema. *Jhinder Bandi* ignited the age-old debate among the Bengali audience as to who was the better actor, Uttam or Soumitra.

*Jhinder Bandi* dealt with kin rivalry unfolding into a bitter drama of betrayal and killing, while *Jotugriha* portrayed marital discord in a subtly nuanced way at a time when divorce and separation were not common themes in Indian films. Adapted from a poignant short story, Tapan maintained his style of simplistic linear narration but added interesting subplots to take the story forward. What makes this film so unforgettable? The sense of a void and the relentless depression at the end of it. The film had no villains, none with any negative shades and yet, there was a couple who drifted apart. Arundhati Devi and Uttam Kumar portrayed the couple with rare restraint. The film created an inescapable sense of helplessness in viewers. Whereas its Hindi remake *Ijazat* directed by Gulzar gave viewers reason to believe that the marriage was ruined due to the presence of a third person.

*Sagina Mahato* is Tapan's most polemical film. Dilip Kumar as Sagina was fantastic, quite a departure from his otherwise tragic romantic roles. The film raised a number of pertinent questions about the failures of trade union movements when Bengal was reeling under Naxalism. Tapan championed the struggles of the common man and his triumph over his situation in this film too. Shot between *Aponjon* and *Ekhoni*, the two films of his *Calcutta Trilogy*, *Sagina Mahato* is in a sense an attempt to break away from the lyricism inherent in most of Tapan's films. It paved the way for more dark films in the future—*Adalat O Ekti Meye*, *Atanka* and *Antardhan*.

The conviction that an individual could brave all odds made Tapan unpopular with some of his friends and critics whose political ideology and beliefs prized community over the individual. The spirit of individualism was propagated most successfully in Tapan's Hindi film *Ek Doctor Ki Maut*. The film was based on the true story of a brilliant doctor-cum-scientist whose inventions went unrecognised due to political and bureaucratic machinations that plague our scientific community. Since it was produced by NFDC, Tapan had the liberty to experiment within the film's narrative limits. What emerged was a very sensitive depiction of a bitter reality that cripples the echelons of academia in India even today.

***

Consider the following categories in the National Film Awards of India: Best Feature Film, Second Best Feature Film, Best Direction and Best Bengali Feature Film. In these categories, up to 2016, Tapan and his films were awarded 13 times, second only to Ray's tally of 24. Buddhadeb Dasgupta, Mrinal Sen and Rituparno Ghosh were each awarded nine times in these categories. Apart from these 13, Tapan's films won numerous other awards so it is strange that he has not received any serious attention from film scholars in India. To the general, educated audience, he remained a beloved film-maker for a very long stretch of his career. His films continue to be liked by many in the new generation. However, due to the abysmal condition of film restoration and preservation in India, some of his films are no longer available. Many have been damaged to such an extent that the technical expertise in cinematography and editing is no longer visible in its original form. So it is a struggle for me to highlight his work (or for that matter anyone else's facing the same fate) and discuss his films with readers who may not even get a chance to view them. Even if they watch Tapan's films in their current condition, the things worth admiring in them are fading away due to lack of preservation. This is why it saddened me to rewatch Tapan's available films for the purpose of writing this book.

*The Cinema of Tapan Sinha* is a tribute to Tapan Sinha, the film-maker who was neglected by his *Aponjon*, his 'own people' for whom he made all his films. If these pages inspire people to study his work in greater detail and with sustained interest, I will consider my efforts a success. If this book prompts the urge to restore his films into modern technical formats, that will be a welcome bonus. After all, Tapan always believed in speaking only through his films.

## REFERENCES

[1] Amitava Nag, 'The Forgotten, Our Very "Own"', *Silhouette Magazine*, 2 December 2014, https://learningandcreativity.com/tapan-sinha-the-forgotten-our-very-own/ accessed on 15 March 2018

[2] Siddhartha Kumar Ghosh, 'A Film-maker Extraordinary', Tapan Sinha: A Tribute, *Cine Central*, 2 October 2009, p. 46

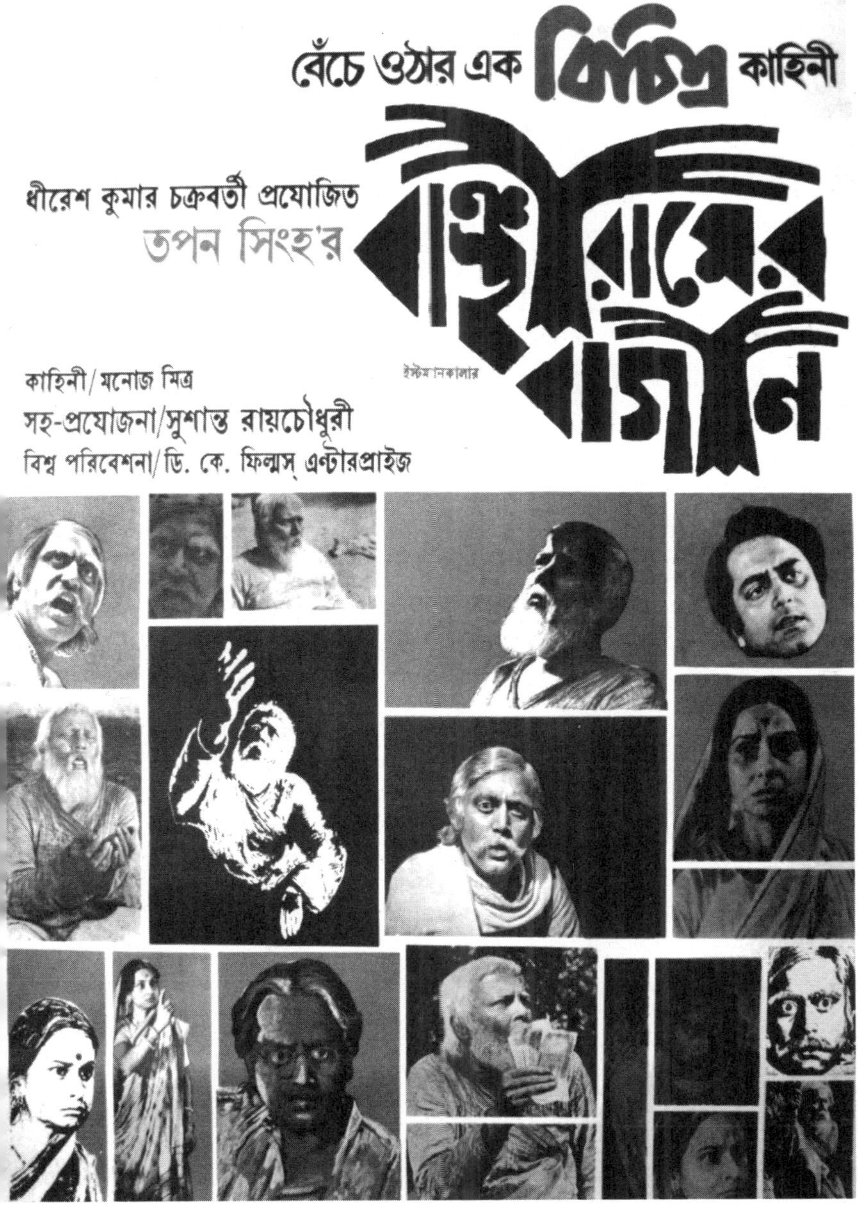
বেঁচে ওঠার এক বিচিত্র কাহিনী
ধীরেশ কুমার চক্রবর্তী প্রযোজিত
তপন সিংহ'র
বাঞ্ছারামের বাগান
ইস্টম্যানকালার
কাহিনী/মনোজ মিত্র
সহ-প্রযোজনা/সুশান্ত রায়চৌধুরী
বিশ্ব পরিবেশনা/ডি. কে. ফিল্মস্ এন্টারপ্রাইজ

# The Initial Years

Sahibganj district has a rich and interesting history dating back centuries during which a number of rulers reigned over it. While the link with Santhal Parganas associates it with a particular history of revolution, it became a seat of power due to Rajmahal, which was once the capital of Bengal province. Rajmahal gained prominence after Mughal rule in Bengal was established in the late 16th century. It was the capital of the all-important Bengal province for a while (on two occasions), and later, it was here that Bengal's Nawab Siraj-ud-Daula was captured during his flight from the British after he lost the Battle of Plassey in 1757. Rajmahal continued to remain an important town even during British rule though its fortunes declined after the emergence of Calcutta and Dhaka as the major administrative cities of the time in Bengal.

The Sinhas had a zamindari in Rajmahal. Where they came from and when are unknown, but in late 19th-century Greater Bengal, they were considered quite a wealthy family. It is also unclear as to when and why the Sinhas let go of their zamindari in Rajmahal and settled in Hilora. Hilora was a small, quaint place, which could be approached from two sides—Murarai Station in Birbhum and Jangipur

Station in Murshidabad. Shifting from Rajmahal shrunk the zamindari though it was big enough to sustain the family at that time.

Tridibesh Chandra Sinha was the head of the Sinha family from the early days of the 20th century. He rebuilt the joint family's economy after they moved to Hilora. Having lost his father at a young age, he had to take the reins of the extended family firmly in his hands. An upright person, he was interested in Sanskrit literature and he was also an able administrator whose strengths were hard work, perseverance, truthfulness and a rare ability to treat people with empathy and compassion. A major part of the family's zamindari was in the Santhal Parganas, but this was nothing in comparison to what they had left behind in Rajmahal.

A handsome man with strikingly fair skin, Tridibesh Chandra was married to Pramila Sundari Devi, a cultured woman herself. She came from an affluent family with a progressive outlook, her maternal grandfather being Rama Prasanna Sinha, the elder brother of Lord S.P. Sinha. Lord Sinha, as he was popularly known, was the first Indian to become the Advocate General of Bengal in 1905. He was also the first Indian to enter the Governor General's Executive Council in 1909 before being elected as the President of the Indian National Congress in 1915. The family was close to the Tagore family and Santiniketan, which naturally helped Pramila Devi to imbibe a rich cultural heritage.

Tagore's songs and dance dramas were performed in her household and Pramila Devi submerged herself in them from an early age. Her father, Brajendra Ghosh Hazra, was a music connoisseur as well. A zamindar himself, Hazra was a devout practitioner of Indian classical music and he could play a number of instruments. This fusion of Rabindra

Sangeet and Indian classical music created a very rich musical base for Pramila Devi.

Tridibesh Chandra and Pramila Devi had four daughters and two sons: Pushparani, Usharani, Barsharani, Gitanjali, Sachindra Kumar and Tapan. Tapan was born in a rented house in Bhawanipore, Kolkata, on Thursday, 2 October 1924. It was 17 Ashwin 1331 in the Bengali calendar and more importantly, Chaturthi, the Fourth Day of Bengal's biggest festival, Durga Puja. In spite of his affluence, Tridibesh Chandra led a relatively simple and austere life. He was a follower of Mahatma Gandhi and had a number of *charkha*s (spinning wheels) at his house. While he was growing up, Tapan watched his family members spinning the *charkha* in the afternoons, a practice he had to follow along with his younger sister Gita. For the younger members of the family, Tridibesh Chandra had smaller *charkha*s, but the diktat was clear. The family used to organise elaborate Durga Puja and Kali Puja celebrations, which were also occasions for assimilating the village people and folk culture into their life. The time he spent in the village instilled a spontaneous love for Nature in Tapan. His observant mind soaked up the details of village life to perfection, memories of which he would recreate much later in his films on rural Bengal.

Sensitive as he was about his father's strict rules, Tapan found plenty of qualities to admire in his father while he was growing up. The Durga idol for Durga Puja used to be built in their house. The painters who came to paint the idols and dress them up in majestic colours were all Muslims. Even in his old age, Tapan could remember a scene—the time of drawing Ma Durga's eyes, an auspicious ritual on the day of Mahalaya. The lead painter would close his eyes for a silent prayer, calm his mind and only then pick up the brush to paint the deity's eyes.

Young Tapan was attached to his father though he was a bit fearful of his strong character and firm attitude. Tapan was in awe of his father's knowledge of Sanskrit and his fine poetic sensibility. During their travels through the forests of Santhal Parganas, Tapan could sense his father's softer side. At night, lying on their makeshift bed, Tridibesh Chandra would recite Kalidasa's epic poem, *Kumãrasambhava* (The Birth of the War God) and the lyrical *Meghadütam* (The Cloud Messenger). He would then explain the poems to young Tapan in simple language, unknowingly training his son in the basics of lyrical poetics. He also instilled an appreciation for Nature in Tapan. Tridibesh Chandra translated the *Durga Stob* (chants about Durga's glory) from Sanskrit to Bengali so that his children would understand them. As an inquisitive child, Tapan did not find the chant a pleasant one. He would question how worshippers could demand so much from the mother goddess!

Tridibesh Chandra had an attractive personality and a magnanimous nature. He was always supportive of his dependents and extended family which banked on him or assisted him. Man's courage to confront the unpleasant realities of life was depicted many times by Tapan in his films. Siddhartha Kumar Ghosh suspects that Tridibesh Chandra's image was at work in Tapan's subconscious mind.

Pramila Devi had a very sweet voice and used to sing Rabindranath Tagore's songs at night while putting her children to sleep. She successfully passed on this musical legacy—her children were all gifted singers in their own right. A young Tapan would particularly remember his mother's rendition of "Jotobar Alo Jwalate Chai" (As Many Times As I Try to Light a Candle) and "Keno Chokher Jole Bhijiye Dilem Na?" (Why Didn't I Moisten it with My Tears?). Much later, in his film *Ekhoni* (Right Now), Tapan used some verses of the latter song, straight from the nostalgic remembrances of his mother's singing sessions in their house at night.

Tapan was a natural singer though he was never trained in music formally. He would listen to his mother and to the music teachers who taught his sisters. Most of his colleagues—actors, technicians and crew members—all agree that he could have done well as a singer had he followed that path. The sense of *taal* (rhythm) and *laya* (tempo) was ingrained in Tapan from an early age. During the *sandhya-arati* (evening prayer) of Durga Puja, he would play the *kaansi*, (circular bronze plate) used as a musical accompaniment for the *dhaak* (Indian percussion instrument like the drum). In a few years, he became an expert in the instrument and developed a distinct style. A couple of years later, when he visited his ancestral home during Durga Puja and started playing the *kaansi* before even entering the house, his mother recognised his style and guessed correctly that it was Tapan who had come home for the holidays.

Pramila Devi's singing acumen and Tridibesh Chandra's penchant for the written word were formative influences on Tapan's artistic sensibility. There were two other influences as well—his maternal grandfather Brajendra Ghosh Hazra's command of Indian classical music nurtured Tapan's interest in the same and effectively helped him years later, when he started composing music for his films. The other major influence was Usharani Devi, his elder sister with whom he spent his formative years.

# Growing up in Bhagalpur

In 1933, Tapan relocated to his elder sister Usharani Ghosh's household in Bhagalpur. His brother-in-law, Manindra Chandra Ghosh, was a well-respected lawyer practising at the Bhagalpur court. He had a philanthropic side to him as well. During his five-decade-long career, he financially helped around 8,000 students to appear for the Matriculation Examination. Bhagalpur was a culturally rich town with an impressive education system. Tridibesh Chandra was very fond of his youngest son and wanted Tapan to receive a proper education, which Hilora was unable to provide. Usharani and Manindra Chandra were very close to Tridibesh Chandra and he would occasionally visit Bhagalpur and stay with his daughter and son-in-law for long spells. His close relationship with them and the advantages Bhagalpur offered as a seat of learning prompted Chandra to pack his young son off to Usharani's home. Usharani also had a daughter who was younger than Tapan. Tapan was lucky to receive both sisterly love and motherly affection from Usharani.

Siddhartha Kumar Ghosh, Usharani's son, explains: "My mother brought him from her father's place to Bhagalpur, then a British Indian city where excellent facilities including education were available. My maternal grandfather had large landed property and was the *Karta* (head of the joint family or clan). He loved Sanskrit literature. He had a good grasp of the law and was invited to the court often as a jury member. He was a culturally inclined person and his circle of friends included Dada Thakur (Sarat Chandra Pandit), a well-known composer of rhymes, a critic and publisher of literary magazines. Durga Puja and Kali Puja were celebrated at his home every year with great fanfare. Yet, he decided to send his youngest son, Tapan, to Bhagalpur, detaching him from the traditional home with a vision of charting out a good future for him. When I look back at the time my children were of that age, I realise how difficult it would have been for me to live without them. I understand this even more when I handle my grandchild who is at a tender age.

"Tapan's journey came about thanks to my maternal grandfather's strength of character and his complete faith in my mother whom he loved most for her ability to rise to the occasion when life demanded extraordinary empathy and truthfulness. He also had faith in my father, a lawyer and freedom fighter who led a simple life in spite of his large inheritance and zamindari. My father had a quest for knowledge, great admiration for the English language and literature besides being deeply involved in philanthropy. My mother's leanings towards aesthetics, mainly literature and music, and her quest for a good lifestyle—a fusion of Indian and Western, assured Chandra of the right environment for my Chhoto Mama (Tapan) to grow. And so, Tapan arrived in Bhagalpur city, which he would remember and describe as his home in all his interviews."

Usharani was a woman with a rare spirit and wisdom. In Bhagalpur, she had designed her house as a fusion of

Eastern and Western patterns daring to embed modernity within the folds of tradition. She also participated in India's freedom struggle in the 1930s and was an active member of the progressive women's team who rejected foreign goods and gathered in front of shops to persuade potential buyers to do the same. Usharani took vocal music lessons at home and so did her elder daughter who was almost the same age as Tapan. Usharani also hosted soirees for musicians visiting the city and invited music lovers to her home. Living in his sister's house, Tapan was able to imagine a world filled with aesthetic joy where literature, music and harmonious human relationships coexist. His proximity to the beauty of nature here including the ethereal Ganga left an indelible mark on his creative process—the reason why outdoor-based themes prevailed in his early films. Tapan's relationship with his elder sister, one of compassion and love, is aptly reflected in *Safed Haathi*, *Ek Je Chhilo Desh* and *Didi*.

In Bhagalpur, Tapan was admitted to the Durgacharan M.E. School in Class IV. The school had classes up to Class VII at that time and was founded by a group of expatriate Bengalis in Bhagalpur. It maintained a high standard of education. The atmosphere was conducive to learning and soon, Tapan started to acquire a broader view of life. The school's headmaster, Surendranath Gangopadhyay, a musician and writer himself, was a relative of the great Bengali litterateur, Sarat Chandra Chattopadhyay, who had spent some time at Bhagalpur. Parts of many of Sarat Chandra's novels are set in the city. Apart from Sarat Chandra, the other great Bengali writer who made Bhagalpur his home was Balaichand Mukhopadhyay (Banaphool).

At school, Gangopadhyay inculcated the habit of reciting poetry in his pupils. Before the daily morning prayer prior to classes, he would play his violin religiously. The headmaster made a lasting impression on Tapan since he was the one who introduced him to the treasure trove of Bengali literature—the works of Rabindranath Tagore. However, the initiation was an accident. One day, Dwijen Babu, the geometry teacher, was on leave. The headmaster came to teach the class as a substitute and instead of discussing geometry, read out portions from a volume of Tagore's verses to the students. To the bewilderment of the entire class, he recited "Puratan Bhritya" (The Old Servant), "Dui Bigha Jami" (Two Yards of Land) and some of Tagore's other famous poems. Henceforth reading Tagore became the order of the day for the geometry class. The headmaster would explain Tagore's nuanced language, which was simple yet profound. Not only did he discuss almost all the stories from *Katha o Kahini* (Words and Tales) but more importantly, he helped his pupils to develop a love for literature. It was only seven days before the examination that he allowed them to study geometric theorems and their corollaries!

By Class VII, Tapan had already internalised the essence of Tagore's "Urvashi" (The Divine Dancer) and "Nirjhorer Swapnabhanga" (The Awakening of the Sleeping Stream). Tagore's works became Tapan's light-bearer, the source of creative energy and solace in his life in times of crises. While the headmaster introduced Tagore to Tapan, the arithmetic teacher, Binoy Bhushan Chatterjee (fondly referred to as Binu-da), would read out excerpts from Sarat Chandra's *Sreekanto*, which was partly set in Bhagalpur, to his students. This gifted teacher could sing well, play the flute and tabla and was an impressive cricket player too. However, Tapan took flute lessons not from him, but from Naresh Babu who would come by every Saturday, bringing along bamboo flutes to train the boys. Learning and creativity were an integral part of this environment, which fostered liberal ideas and helped pupils to develop a holistic view of the self in conjunction with Nature. Tapan passed out of the school in 1940 and enrolled for Intermediate curriculum in the science stream.

The 11 years Tapan spent at Bhagalpur were a defining period in his life. His vision was enlarged thanks to his teachers who inculcated a passion for creativity and a strict sense of discipline in him. This stayed with him all his life. Bhagalpur being a town of considerable political importance as compared to his ancestral village, Tapan carried away two seminal memories from there. Around 1936–1937, Mahatma Gandhi visited Bhagalpur to address a public gathering. Tapan, then a Class VI student, attended the meeting along with his friends. The crowd was much larger than expected and soon pandemonium broke loose, resulting in a massive stampede. Tapan was wounded—a few of his ribcage bones were fractured and he was taken home in an unconscious state. Things took a turn for the worse as he started throwing up blood and he had to be shifted to Calcutta for treatment.

It took three months for Tapan to recover and return to Bhagalpur to resume his studies. Years later, in 1948, Tapan was in Calcutta when he heard the news about Gandhi's assassination. Travelling on a tram that fateful day, Tapan realised that not a single passenger was speaking and the conductor was also not asking them for the fare. It felt as if the whole city had slipped into a trance. Tridibesh Chandra and Manindra Chandra were both Gandhi's followers and they used to wear khadi garments. After Gandhi's assassination, Tridibesh Chandra even observed *asouch*, the

Hindu religious practice of restricting non-vegetarian food intake after the demise of a blood relative.

When Tapan was in Class IX, he had the privilege of seeing another great Indian leader up close—Netaji Subhas Chandra Bose. Netaji's speech in Urdu was etched on Tapan's impressionable mind. Netaji's bold and courageous personality, and his warning to the British Empire thrilled Tapan, and he remained a Netaji follower ever since.

The Bhagalpur period was of particular significance because Tapan's first encounters with cinema happened there. At that time, Bhagalpur had only one cinema hall called Picture Palace, which used to screen foreign films every Friday and Sunday. Tapan enjoyed watching the adventure films screened there including the likes of *Tarzan* and *King Kong*. Once he became a teenager, Tapan developed a fondness for the classics that were at his disposal. This affinity for the classics sprung from his teacher, Gurudas Babu, who used to teach both English and history at Tapan's school. Gurudas was a favourite among the students because of his animated lectures, which teemed with cross references to different art forms.

Gurudas suggested the students watch the film version of Charles Dickens's *A Tale of Two Cities* while teaching a class on the French Revolution. The film was being screened at the local cinema at the time and viewing it changed Tapan's perception of life altogether. Tapan was enamoured with the actor Ronald Colman who played Sydney Carton in *A Tale of Two Cities*. Watching classic English films, predominantly Hollywood ones, became a constant for him. Even in the later stages of his life, when he was virtually confined to the indoors, this continued. He would occasionally call his favourite actors like Nirmal Kumar, Soumitra Chatterjee and Manoj Mitra to watch the films with him and discuss the various techniques used in them (including acting).

Watching Hollywood classics helped him to appreciate the conventional linear narrative structure of storytelling and also taught him valuable lessons about the importance of acting in cinema. Actors like Gary Cooper, Clark Gable, Betty Davis and others impressed Tapan with their histrionic ability. His immersion in Hollywood ensured that when he eventually became a film-maker, acting remained a vital cog in his machinery. Sticking to Hollywood methodology, he would rehearse with the actors in his films—both amateurs and experienced ones. Every actor associated with his films talks about how Tapan would enact parts of the role himself for the actor to understand the temperament of the character and ensure a perfect delivery in the shot.

In 1941, when Tapan was in the first year of college, a shocking piece of news shook Bhagalpur—that of the demise of Rabindranath Tagore. Tapan had become an ardent admirer of Tagore by then. Absorbing the news was very difficult for him and the entire Bengali community of Bhagalpur. A commemorative meeting was organised at the assembly of the Church Missionary Society (CMS) High School. CMS was located next to the old premises of the Durgacharan M.E. School. The Principal, Mr Hartford, who was very popular with the students, gave a heartfelt rendition of Tagore's immortal poem, "Hey Bandhu Biday" (Farewell, Dear Friend). No one could possibly remember a departed soul with such dignity and respect. Many years later, in his film *Wheel Chair* (1994), Tapan would infuse a great deal of compassion and poise in a crucial death scene, digging deep into his own experience of hearing the former Principal's restrained tribute.

Tapan's involvement with cinema became more active and direct after he acquired his Matriculate degree and enrolled in the Intermediate science stream. He continued to watch Hollywood classics but there was more purpose in those viewings. He became interested in learning the various techniques of film-making. This motivated him to read the interviews of important directors featured in all the English magazines he could lay his hands on.

Reading about the likes of John Ford, William Wyler, Carol Reed, Fred Zinnemann and Billy Wilder helped him to relate to their cinema. Soon, the entire process of film-making began to seem like a great adventure to him. Growing up in Bhagalpur and spending his childhood in his village home had made him a natural adventurer. This thirst for adventure is reflected in the diversity of subjects he chose. Seldom did he pick similar themes for his films. He also tried his hand at genres ranging from the classics to the contemporary, from vast outdoor locales to the interiors of middle-class homes.

Tapan would take his camera to mountains, jungles, the banks of rivers and the seashore. Though he was keen on studying the arts, Tridibesh Chandra ordered him to take up science. He had no choice but to obey his father. Pursuing science, however, helped him in the long run when he joined New Theatres Studio after completing his studies.

পরিবেশক · ছায়াবাণী লিঃ

জতুগৃহ
কাহিনী • সুবোধ ঘোষ
পরিচালনা : তপন সিংহ

# The Move to the Big City

In 1943, Tapan left Bhagalpur and went to Calcutta to join the Engineering College at Jadavpur, which went on to become part of the famous Jadavpur University in 1955. While he was a student at Jadavpur, Tapan developed the habit of watching foreign classics more regularly. It almost turned into an addiction. At the time, he had no specific preferences—he simply binged on Hollywood films. However, he was particular about the Indian and Bengali films he chose to watch during those years.

Engineering didn't interest Tapan for long and he abandoned it in the first year itself. He switched to a Bachelor of Science in Physics Honours and graduated in 1945. In Calcutta, Tapan stayed at the Presidency Boarding House on Harrison Road, which was renamed Mahatma Gandhi Road shortly after. During his stay, Tapan was influenced by Dr. Sudhindra Nath Sanyal, a close family friend. Dr. Sanyal was the son of Baikuntha Nath Sanyal, the author of *Sri Sri Ramakrishna Leelamrita* and a devout disciple of Sri Ramakrishna Paramhansa. A leading scientist, Dr. Sanyal had received the Minto Gold Medal from the School of Tropical Medicine for his research. His early research was on oral contraceptives and later, he made a significant contribution to the research on cancer therapy. He was accepted by Pramila Devi as her godson and played mentor to Tapan who was new to the big city.

Calcutta was reeling from the impact of Gandhi's Quit India movement in 1942 and the aftermath of the Great Bengal Famine of 1943–1944. It was during this troubled time that Tapan found the lure of cinema too powerful to ignore. He was eager to pursue higher studies and in 1946, he found himself at the gates of the iconic New Theatres Studio. The decision to join films was not a sudden whim or a stroke of luck. Tapan had mulled over it deeply before approaching New Theatres, which was at the helm of its creativity. Tapan lacked the courage to share his plans with his father, but he took his mother into confidence.

Jagadish Bhattacharya was a manager at New Theatres and a close acquaintance of Dr. Sanyal's. Dr. Sanyal wrote to Bhattacharya about Tapan and became instrumental in inducting Tapan into the Studio. Having studied Physics, Tapan found it logical to consider the Sound Department as his entry point. During an informal interview, the technicians at the Department dissuaded Tapan from joining the film industry due to its inherent uncertainties. However, Tapan was steadfast in his decision and ultimately, he was offered the post of Associate Sound Technician on a monthly salary of Rs. 70.

At New Theatres, Tapan's formal training in the technique of cinema started. The Sound Department had a number of technical stalwarts including Mukul Bose (legendary sound recordist and brother of film director, Nitin Bose), Loken Basu and Atul Chatterjee as well as Bani Dutta, under whom Tapan joined as an Associate. The informal atmosphere at the Studio allowed Tapan to learn from all these gifted technicians.

New Theatres was the seat of creative genius of the Bengali film industry. Bimal Roy was yet to migrate to Bombay taking along with him highly talented individuals like Hrishikesh Mukherjee, Nabendu Ghosh and Asit Sen. Roy had already shot to fame by then, thanks to his artistically nuanced and commercially successful Bengali film, *Udayer Pathe* (Towards the Light, 1944). Tapan got a chance to observe Roy closely while he was at work on the sets of *Humrahi* (the Hindi version of *Udayer Pathe*). Roy found in Tapan an attentive learner with a creative and imaginative mind. Tapan borrowed the film's script from Roy and read it thoroughly several times, an exercise that helped him later when he started writing scripts for his own films. To Tapan's advantage, Roy gave him the space to discuss the film's script and share his views freely.

Working at New Theatres fuelled Tapan's hunger to make his own films. He started writing scripts—the first was based on Ernest Hemingway's 1927 short story, *The Killers*. Incidentally, the first film version of this story was made at the same time (in 1946), starring Burt Lancaster in his debut role, and William Conrad, Ava Gardner and others. Tapan's script did not have many takers among his friends, but that did not dampen his spirits. He continued writing and took up both Western and Bengali stories. Tapan had an unforgettable experience during this period: "I had a brilliant plot in mind, a crime drama. I named it *Kara Prachir* (Jail Wall). At that time, there was a Hollywood hero named Rod Cameron who was 6 feet 5 inches tall. I had actually visualised an actor in that mould. But a person of that stature is difficult to get. Then one day, suddenly, I found a person on Chowringhee who matched all my required criteria—an immensely tall and healthy figure.

I was about to talk to him, but I restrained myself since I had no resources but the script. So, I couldn't actually get myself introduced to him. However, much later, we came to know each other quite well, and I was fortunate to receive his love and affection. The name of that person is Satyajit Ray."[1]

After working for two years at New Theatres, Tapan moved to a new studio called Calcutta Movietone, which was in the formative stage at that time. Tapan's mentor, Bani Dutta, had already moved there as Chief Sound Recordist. The responsibilities of setting up a studio from scratch helped Tapan to grow as a technically creative person. His mastery over the cinematic medium can largely be attributed to his years at New Theatres and Calcutta Movietone.

At Calcutta Movietone, Tapan got a chance to work independently for the first time. He worked in Satyen Bose's debut film, *Paribartan* (Change, 1949), as the sole sound recordist and followed it up with Bose's next, *Barjatri* (The Groom's Party), a year later. Around the same time, noted cinematographer-cum-director Ajoy Kar was shooting his detective thriller *Jighansha* (Revenge), which was based on Arthur Conan Doyle's *The Hound of the Baskervilles*. The nature of the film's plot allowed Tapan to experiment and he tried incorporating different background sounds with particular emphasis on creating effects with echo iteratively. This was a brand new experience for the audience. The fraternity of technicians too appreciated it greatly.

This success paved the way for more work for Tapan. Then came a watershed moment—French legend Jean Renoir arrived in Kolkata in the latter half of 1950 to shoot his film, *The River* (1951). Satyajit Ray met him and discussed in detail his ideas and plans for *Pather Panchali* (Song of the Little Road, 1955), which remains one of Indian cinema's most influential and impactful events till date. *The River* plays an important role in the history of Indian cinema. Bansi Chandragupta worked as Art Director in the film and Ray and Subrata Mitra as assistants. This triumvirate joined forces to come up with the masterpiece, *Pather Panchali* in 1955.

Many technicians and aspiring film-makers met Renoir when he was in Calcutta to understand his philosophy and seek his guidance. Tapan was introduced to Renoir's unit and to Charles Poulton, the sound engineer, through a friend. The unit had brought along a magnetic sound-recording machine manufactured by Western Electric, which was the first of its kind. Tapan was interested to learn more about the technique of magnetic tape recording and wanted to join the unit in installing the machine. Generous man that he was, Bani Dutta, Tapan's boss at Calcutta Movietone who knew about Tapan's dream of becoming a film-maker, made this wish come true by approving Tapan's leave application for six months. Tapan joined Renoir's unit and worked there for a month, after which he had to leave Calcutta to be with his widowed mother.

In 1949, Tridibesh Chandra Sinha passed away before he could witness his son's creative exploits that went on to enthrall audiences for decades to come. For Tapan, his father's death was a great loss. Not only because he had shared a close bond with his father and had inherited a lyrical sensibility from him, but more importantly, because he had never discussed his film-making ambitions with his parent fearing he would reject them summarily.

## REFERENCES

[1]Tapan Sinha, *Chalachchitra Ajibon*, Ed: Shamik Bandopadhyay, Dey's Publishing, 2009, p.12 [Translation by the author]

# London Calling

Tapan felt a deep sense of respect and love for his father from his early childhood. The move to Bhagalpur did not dull these feelings and Tapan missed his father's company terribly. In Calcutta, when Tapan was literally sucked into the realm of cinema, he was unsure how his father would react to this venture. Tridibesh Chandra had high hopes for Tapan and wanted his son to pursue a more traditional academic career. This was the primary reason that had motivated him to send Tapan to study at Bhagalpur, which had a better academic environment than their native village. After joining New Theatres, Tapan had confided in his mother about his film-making plans, but he had decided to wait for the right time to bring it up with his father. Chandra's sudden demise shocked Tapan. He had to rush back from Renoir's set to be with his widowed mother and the extended family, which had suddenly woken up to the fact of having lost a guardian who used to look after every aspect of their lives.

Tridibesh Chandra was the younger of two brothers, and the elder one had passed away years ago. Chandra's ethic in his home had been to treat everyone with equality and fairness. Members of the families of both brothers lived together in the house. After Chandra's death, it was not at all easy for the large family to manage day-to-day life—from financial to operational matters to coping with their grief. One of the first casualties on the home front was the Durga Puja celebrations, which stopped the year Chandra passed away.

A restless Tapan returned to Calcutta after a few months, but he had lost interest in the city and in his life there. The job at Calcutta Movietone alone was not enough to keep him motivated and engaged enough to combat his grief. Tapan was disappointed that Renoir's unit had left town and gone back to Europe. However, he did get a chance to engage with Renoir's film after his return to Calcutta.

Patricia Walters who starred in *The River* was born and brought up in Calcutta. Renoir's team found her while scouting for the film's cast. Walters went on to play Harriet, the protagonist of the film. Tapan got to know that Walters's voiceover was to be rerecorded. She was still in the city and Tapan was entrusted with the work. He improvised, making use of his work experience, and constructed a makeshift sound enclosure to record the voiceover afresh. The recording was sent to Hollywood for sound processing, but unfortunately it was found to be unusable due to over-damping. Tapan realised that the sound enclosure had not been a proper one and hence the quality of the recording had suffered. This was his last technical association with *The River*.

However, Tapan kept in touch with a few crew members of Renoir's unit including Charles Poulton, the sound engineer. Tapan shared his wish to visit the prestigious Pinewood Studios and learn sound techniques there with Poulton. After Poulton spoke to the concerned authorities, Tapan received the necessary approvals. George Rearden who was managing the India wing of the famous Rank organisation at that time, was an acquaintance of Tapan's. Rank was the owner of Pinewood Studios. Rearden too helped Tapan to get to Pinewood.

With both these references in hand, Tapan landed in the UK in the summer of 1950 and stayed there for over a year to learn the craft of film-making. It was a mixed experience for him. He reminisced: "Those one-and-a-half years were basically a waste for me. I did not learn anything new to add to the range of experiences I already had ... However, the most precious thing that I learnt during my stay in England was discipline—of work and thought. That helped me tremendously in the days to come. While writing a script for a film, I made sure not to entertain complex thoughts, which might be difficult to capture and would lead to a waste of raw stock. In a country like ours, where we have to constantly make films on a limited budget, this discipline is absolutely essential."[1]

In an interview with director Rituparno Ghosh, Tapan elaborated: "What I liked at Pinewood was the way they administered everything—how they would maximise an individual's efficiency and use it for the work, and then leave him on his own after that. I learnt that you can work in a film like you do in a time-bound job. I feel my biggest learning there was to understand that creativity doesn't necessarily mean bohemianism; there is scope for substantial discipline in your creative faculties also. I used to think that if I ever got to work in my own way back home, I would introduce this in my film unit. Everyone will come at 10 a.m. and leave at 5 p.m., just like in any other office job. I did follow it rigidly. My unit had lunch break at 1 p.m. and I stuck to it even if a shot remained incomplete.

"Looking back, I think most of the artists and crew members who worked with me were preconditioned with this working pattern and the results were always good for me ... Many say that you have to mentally arrange and organise the work that you are planning to do. To me it is equally important to execute that blueprint within the stipulated timeline. If each individual member can plan the day's work within the seven hours from 10 a.m. to 5 p.m. and the entire film's work in 30 days (or whatever number that is set), the execution becomes easy and uncomplicated. In films, the budget will spill over the moment the number of days increases. I believe that if we can control the work time effectively then we can definitely control the financial overheads."[2]

Any colleague of Tapan's would vouch for this discipline of thought and execution, which helped individual members to plan their respective tasks and benefitted the unit as a whole. Nilanjan Bhattacharya, an independent documentary film-maker who worked as Tapan's assistant, said: "I observed at close quarters how disciplined Tapan Sinha's way of working was. But it was not a suffocating discipline that he would impose on the unit. It was a very natural one because sufficient time was devoted during the pre-production phase wherein the complete production plan was laid out in detail. It was not that there were no changes to that plan. Even during those initial planning days, there used to be room for making minor changes later on ... Working in his team I could understand the importance of a proper and realistic shooting schedule ... In my experience, there were only a few days of extension in the schedule due to unavoidable reasons.

"Generally, during indoor shoots he would pack up half an hour before the shift's end time. This was because the day's stipulated work used to be over by that time. But to achieve that, I never observed any hurry on his part. He would give ample time to the cameraman to configure the light settings, to the make-up man to work on the make-up, to the actors to rehearse their lines. If required, he never shied away from shooting multiple retakes as well. There was a smooth, eloquent rhythm to his working style. I understand why he insisted I learn feature film management. I realise that feature film management is not the job of the production manager or the assistant director alone, the main person is actually the film director."[3]

Apart from the work ethic which helped Tapan in his film-making career, the other benefit of his tenure at Pinewood was the opening up of a plethora of world cinema before him. In Bhagalpur and Calcutta, the only foreign films he could watch were the Hollywood classics—products of the great Hollywood 'studio system'. Hence, the likes of John Ford, William Wyler, Carol Reed, Billy Wilder and other Hollywood greats of the thirties and forties had captured Tapan's attention. His London stay helped him to discover world cinema and its staggering range: "I did benefit from a different perspective. While staying there, I had the opportunity to watch a lot of European movies. It was remarkable; as if an entirely new horizon in the world of cinema had opened up ... The British Film Institute had started functioning at that time ... There was a collection of film stills there. We used to study these images and learn about composition."[4] Roberto Rossellini's *Rome, Open City* (1945) and *Paisan* (1946), Robert Flaherty's *Nanook of the North* (1922) and *Louisiana Story* (1948) were a few of the notable films that Tapan watched in London.

However, the stay at London, where he had to share a hostel room with three other friends from different countries, left him bored. When he was not at Pinewood or watching films at the British Film Institute, he was on the lookout for adventure. One such journey took him to an institute that offered people fencing lessons. Tapan had a good physique and adequate energy to handle the stress of film shoots. So, joining fencing classes was more of an adventure than a necessity for him. It was not just about exploring an unknown physical experience. It showed a state of mind that always welcomed challenges. Tapan may or may not have had plans at that time to make a film involving sword-fighting or fencing. However, when *Jhinder Bandi* (the 1961 Bengali adaptation of *The Prisoner of Zenda*) was being filmed, his own experience in fencing did come in handy.

The London stint was also memorable because of his meetings with two stalwarts in the field of art. One day at lunch, a friend introduced Tapan to Sir Laurence Olivier. Tapan was not prepared for such a surprise. He was an ardent follower of Sir Laurence's acting—in films and on the stage. The two discussed India and theatre—Bengali theatre in particular. Sir Laurence gave him a valuable piece of advice about adapting successful, written plays: "There is nothing called a 'read-only' play. Every one of them can be adapted on stage."[5] A young Tapan knew that any piece of literature could be made into a film as well. In his filmography, we find this reflected in the diversity of subjects he picked as well as in his dependence on and adherence to literature as source material. In an interview with noted film scholar Shamik Bandopadhyay, Tapan elaborated on the reason for picking varied subjects. "After the first seven or eight films, I did stop to think once if I should try to develop a style of my own, but then I thought better, and decided to let my subject matter, my themes determine my style for me. The restless man that I am, I knew I just couldn't stick to a style, and under pressure I could just become repetitive … A Hollywood director would be making a crime thriller one day, a Western immediately after that, and then *How Green Was My Valley*, opening up new horizons continuously. I thought: why don't I try to do something similar? Let me explore several directions, keeping in mind that I had to reach out to the Bengali audience and provide honest entertainment to them."[6]

The second meeting that made Tapan's London period memorable was not as unplanned as the first. The seed of it germinated from a chance encounter with a renowned poet at the University of London. Tapan realised the poet's face was a familiar one, but he was not sure who the person was. Tapan's roommate Philip, who was pursuing his PhD at the University of London, identified the poet as none other than the Nobel laureate T.S. Eliot. Eliot had been awarded the Nobel Prize in Literature only two years ago, in 1948. However, since there was no barrage of publicity surrounding authors at that time, identifying Eliot was no easy task for Indians like Tapan. However, due to his strong inclination towards literature, which developed right from his childhood days thanks to his father's efforts, he happened to be familiar with Eliot's poetry. He decided to pay the poet a visit even if he was not sure what they would talk about. It was a short meeting, but Eliot's conversation and his piercing gaze left an indelible impression on Tapan.

Life in an unfamiliar city soon started taking a toll on Tapan even if his days were filled with activities—working at the studio from morning till afternoon, visiting the British

Film Institute in the evening and watching night shows of classic films. Tapan decided he had had enough—the sophisticated technical equipment and processes in London were a far cry from those in use in India. He realised that he would have to find a way to work with the techniques available in Calcutta. Lingering on in London was pointless.

## REFERENCES

[1] Tapan Sinha, *Chalachchitra Ajibon*, Ed: Shamik Bandopadhyay, Dey's Publishing, 2009, p. 307 [Translation by the author]

[2] Ibid., pp. 362–363 [Translation by the author]

[3] Nilanjan Bhattacharya, 'Tapan Sinha Ebong Feature Film Management', *Silhouette*, Vol. VII, 10 November 2009, pp. 160–161

[4] Tapan Sinha, *Chalachchitra Ajibon*, Ed: Shamik Bandopadhyay, Dey's Publishing, 2009, p. 307 [Translation by the author]

[5] Ibid., p. 82 [Translation by the author]

[6] Ibid., pp. 445–446 [Translation by the author]

তপন সিংহ পরিচালিত
ক্ষণিকের অতিথি
প্রযোজনা
ভোলানাথ রায়

# *Ankush*: A New Beginning

On his return to Calcutta, Tapan found a life of struggle waiting for him. He had written a few scripts since he joined New Theatres. However, none of them could please him, let alone others. Finally, he zeroed in on noted Bengali writer Narayan Ganguly's short story, *Sainik* (The Soldier), which revolves around a zamindar and his pet elephant. Ganguly was a contemporary writer who taught Bengali at a city college. He was writing a biography of the social reformer Raja Ram Mohan Roy at that time.Tapan was greatly moved by his sense of decency and words of encouragement. Ganguly gave Tapan the go ahead to adapt *Sainik* into a film titled *Ankush* (The Hook).

Tapan's penchant for adventure drove him to select *Sainik* for his first film. Till then, outdoor-oriented films had been rare in Bengali cinema and Indian cinema in general. Returning from London after having watched many world classics, Tapan was inspired to make the first outdoor film in Bengali. The film had only one scene on an indoor set, the rest was shot outdoors. The lightweight Arriflex camera was not available at that time and Tapan used a sound-proof Vinten to shoot the film. The camera was heavy and difficult to operate, particularly because of the extensive outdoor shoots and the inexperience of the crew and Tapan himself in handling the camera.

*Ankush* was planned as a double version—in both Bengali and Hindi. Cinematographer Anil Bandopadhyay, an old friend of Tapan's and a constant source of support, pushed him to complete the script, visit producers and start shooting in 1952. Bandopadhyay naturally donned the mantle of cinematographer of *Ankush*. He also went on to handle the camera for all of Tapan's films, apart from *Louhakapat* (Jail Doors), in the fifties. Bimal Mukhopadhyay first came on board Tapan's team as a cinematographer in *Louhakapat*, and he went on to shoot most of Tapan's films through the sixties and seventies.

During the making of *Ankush*, Tapan's friend Bansi Chandragupta took him to meet Satyajit Ray. Tapan knew of Ray as an important, emerging commercial artist and the son of Sukumar Ray, the Bengali writer revered to this day for his unparalleled nonsense rhymes. To his surprise, Tapan discovered that Satyajit Ray was the same person he had seen at Chowringhee a few years back and considered casting in a film that never took off. The two immediately connected because of their shared interest in art and culture. Ray wanted to hear about Tapan's experiences at Pinewood and the advances in cinematic techniques. Ray also shared his dream of making *Pather Panchali* with Tapan. A script-reading session followed and Tapan was blown away by the story's sensitivity, luminous strength and myriad possibilities of cinematic brilliance.

On 19 March 1954, the Bengali version of *Ankush* was released in Uttara, Purabi and Ujjwala halls. For reasons unknown, the film was withdrawn after a week-and-a-half of its release. Even the print was not made available for future reference. This was a big shock for Tapan. His struggle to stay afloat in the merciless world of motion pictures went on. He was hard hit because he and his friends had borne a substantial part of the production costs of *Ankush*. Unfortunately, the Hindi version was never made.

The film, however, got favourable reviews from the critics. Renowned critic Pankaj Dutta (pen name, Souvik), lauded the film in the leading culture magazine, *Desh* (27 March 1954 issue): "Little Pictures is not a well-known production company, no one has heard of a director named Tapan Sinha, yet their film, *Ankush,* is promising for presenting variety with a lot of filmic proficiency ... At a time when it is difficult to make an arresting film even with human heroes and heroines, the idea of making a commercial film with an elephant as the hero not only calls for a remarkably adventurous mind, but more importantly, it reflects the boldness of the director ... Not only with respect to Bengali cinema, but within the context of Indian cinema as well it is difficult to find another example of such a film. It can be safely said that after *Mahaprasthaner Pathe* (Journey to Heaven, dir. Kartick Chattopadhyay, 1952) there has not been a film, which kept us engrossed with such new and refreshingly different content."[1]

The box-office failure of *Ankush* was a severe blow to Tapan, but he realised that it had failed at 'entertaining' the audience, an attribute which was of utmost importance to him. The flop notwithstanding, the conversations Tapan had had with Narayan Ganguly on the social reformers Raja Ram Mohan Roy and Iswar Chandra Vidyasagar left a deep and lasting impact on him. He had great respect for both. Ganguly's analytical references helped him to understand the power of the individual's protest against the system:

"Later on, this belief was reflected in several of my films. The truth is I was never convinced about collective protest against social injustice or causes."[2]

The film's failure left Tapan with a severe financial crunch. The evolving Narasu Studio at Tamil Nadu was looking for a sound technician at that time and they contacted Tapan with a job offer. The remuneration was lucrative, but after mulling over the offer for a few days, Tapan declined it. Calcutta Movietone showed an interest in bringing him back to their sound department as well. However, destiny had other plans in store for him. He was determined to become a film-maker. Suffering the sting of failure was the challenge he had to accept to pursue his dream.

Tapan started the hunt for the next script soon after he snapped out of his depressed state of mind. Sailajananda Mukhopadhyay was an eminent writer and a film-maker who had been associated with New Theatres long before Tapan joined the studio. Tapan had already read Mukhopadhyay's short story, *Krishna*, and decided to change the name to *Upahar* (The Gift) for his film. Unlike *Ankush*, which was mostly set outdoors, *Upahar* was an indoor social drama. The film revolves around a miserly old man named Kangali who values money over human relationships including the one he shares with his motherless daughter, Krishna. Fortunately for Tapan, *Upahar* fared well at the box office and the producers were able to recover part of the costs.

The central character of Kangali was played by Kanu Bandopadhyay in the film. Bandopadhyay was also playing Harihar in Ray's *Pather Panchali* at the time. The two characters were completely different. To Bandopadhyay's credit, he went on to portray both with ease. *Upahar* also featured Uttam Kumar in a pivotal character role, his first in a Tapan Sinha film. Kumar was already in the process of becoming the brightest star of Bengali cinema, with more than 20 films to his name. *Upahar* also starred Nirmal Kumar as the romantic hero opposite a young Sabitri Chatterjee (as Krishna), and Manju Dey as Uttam's on-screen wife. Dey, the wife of Tapan's friend Satyabrata Dey, was a constant source of support in the early days of Tapan's career. She was quite an influential person in the Bengali film industry and helped Tapan to reach his full potential as a film-maker. Manju Dey and Anil Bandopadhyay supported Tapan wholeheartedly during the struggling phase of his career. Nirmal Kumar went on to feature in several of Tapan's films from then on.

Though not comparable to the artistic partnership between Satyajit Ray and Soumitra Chatterjee, the Tapan Sinha-Nirmal Kumar bond is a significant one. Having acted in 14 of Tapan's 31 Bengali films, Nirmal Kumar played the central character in a number of them, starting with *Upahar*. Even when he was no longer playing the hero, he essayed important secondary characters in Tapan's films, including his last-released Bengali film, *Ajab Gayer Ajab Katha* (The Strange Story of a Strange Village, 1998). This was possible mainly because of Tapan's lifelong friendship with him, which went beyond the sets. Nirmal Kumar, Soumitra Chatterjee and Manoj Mitra were regular visitors at Tapan's home during his later years. They would often watch films on Tapan's video player and discuss them. Even during his youth, Tapan used to encourage Kumar to watch Hollywood classics so the two could discuss them in detail. This mentoring was somewhat similar to Ray's mentoring of Soumitra during the latter's formative years as an actor.

*Upahar* was released on 12 August 1955, a fortnight before the release of Ray's first feature film, *Pather Panchali*. *Upahar* bagged the Best Screenplay Prize at the Bengal Film Journalists' Association (BFJA) Awards that year. Most of the other awards went to Ray's masterpiece.

Tapan opted for *Tonsil* (1956), a comedy next. This was adapted from a comic literary series penned by Bibhutibhusan Mukhopadhyay. A prequel called *Barjatri* (The Marriage Procession) directed by Satyen Bose had been released in 1951. Tapan had worked in the sound department of *Barjatri* and since then, the idea of making a comic film had been haunting him. After *Upahar*'s moderate acceptance (the film was not a big box-office success), Tapan gained confidence. The comedy genre was flourishing in Bengali cinema then, riding on great comedians such as Bhanu Bandopadhyay, Jahar Roy, Tulsi Chakraborty and others. *Pasher Bari* (The Neighbour's House, 1952), *Ora Thake Odhare* (They Live on that Side, 1954) and *Saare Chuattor* (Seventy Four-and-a-Half, 1953)—the hugely successful comedies of the early fifties—gave Tapan the necessary zeal to try his hand at the genre. He roped in almost all the top comedians of the day from Bhanu Bandopadhyay, Jahar Roy, and Nripati Chatterjee to Shyam Laha as well as a young Anup Kumar (who later became a comedian of repute). The film also starred Madhabi Mukhopadhyay, as the heroine. She had appeared in a few inconsequential films and was still known as Madhuri. She was acting on the stage at that time. When Tapan launched the search for a heroine for *Tonsil*, he was sure he wanted a relatively unknown face. One of the main criteria for the heroine was that she needed to be extremely slim, almost sickly, to fit into the role. Mukhopadhyay was an ideal pick. *Tonsil* gave her her first big break in films. Fortunately, *Tonsil* went on to fare well and Tapan's directorial acumen was praised by most critics.

On 29 November 1955, the first Secretary of the Communist Party of the Soviet Union, Nikita Khrushchev, and the then Premier of the Soviet Union, Nikolai Bulganin, visited Calcutta to attend a public meeting. It was a courtesy visit and the duo travelled to several Indian cities, paving the way for a strong Indo-Russian bond in the process. Calcutta gave the Soviet leaders a warm welcome and millions greeted them on the streets and sidewalks. It was on this historic day that producer Asit Choudhury suggested Tapan make a film based on Rabindranath Tagore's short story, *Kabuliwala* (The Merchant from Kabul).

## REFERENCES

[1] Tapan Sinha, 'Chhabi Tairir Kahini', Tapan Sinha: A Tribute, *Cine Central*, 2 October 2009, pp. 12–13

[2] Tapan Sinha, *Chalachchitra Ajibon*, Ed: Shamik Bandopadhyay, Dey's Publishing, 2009, p. 86 [Translation by the author]

চারুচিত্র নিবেদিত
রবীন্দ্রনাথের
কাবুলিওয়ালা

# Embarking on Tagore's Stories

Asit Choudhury's proposal pleasantly surprised Tapan. Tagore's stories were yet to be included in the canon of Bengali cinema at that time. Tagore's literature was kept aside as 'intellectual' stuff unsuitable for commercial mainstream cinema. Sarat Chandra Chattopadhyay was the more popular writer among film-makers and producers. Choudhury offered Tapan a modest monthly remuneration of Rs. 300 for the directorial work. For Tapan, money was never the motivation or a deterrent. The opportunity to work on a Tagore story was his primary inspiration. Since his childhood, Tagore had been a singular source of sustenance for him. That apart, the film appealed to him because it had many outdoor scenes (set against the backdrop of Afghanistan) and also a 'non-Bengali' protagonist, a first in Bengali cinema. Tapan would also get to work with a child actor, another first in his career. Working with child actors is difficult for any director and it takes a lot of patience and skill to handle children's moods. The experience he gained from *Kabuliwala* helped Tapan on this front and enabled him to evolve into one of the prominent Bengali film-makers of children's films.

However, the project was far from a cakewalk. Tapan said: "Mr. Charuchandra Bhattacharya was an influential member of the Visva-Bharati Music Board. He was a very conservative Tagore expert. I sent the script of *Kabuliwala* to him and he returned it with a 'no'. I was young then and this infuriated me a lot. I wanted to have a meeting with him to discuss it … It was a rainy day and I could just save my script from being drenched as I reached his place … He told me, 'What do I need to discuss? You have messed it up completely and deviated from Tagore's path.' I insisted that I would read 15–20 minutes of the script and then he could comment. I started reading. After about 15 minutes, I could see tears trickling down the old man's cheeks. He wailed: 'Very good, very good.' I told him, 'Please write this "very good" on the script and sign it.' After this, I returned along with the necessary permissions."[1]

This sorted out the initial hassle but the problem resurfaced on the first day of the shoot: "Charu-da entered the shooting floor and shouted at me: 'You have emotionally blackmailed me … Tagore had written that the money was given to Rahmat by Mini's father. You have changed it to Mini's mother. This is reason enough for getting the script cancelled.' They used to act in such an extreme manner. Fortunately, the problem didn't persist for long. In my experience, the trouble was that they didn't probe deeper into the meanings and created unnecessary controversies. Later, during *Kshudhita Pashan* (The Hungry Stones, 1960) as well, Charu-da objected to a subplot. I told him that it was in Tagore's story but to know that, one had to read between the lines. Frankly, I loved taking on and overcoming this challenge. There was no such resistance when I made *Atithi* (The Guest, 1965)."[2]

Ironically enough, Tapan was later made a member of the Visva-Bharati Music Board. During his tenure, he was instrumental in ensuring that the Hindi film *Dak Ghar* (The Post Office, 1966), directed by Zul Velani, based on Tagore's play with the same name, tided over some of the inconsequential obstacles put forward by the puritan section of the Board.

Tapan roped in sitar maestro Ravi Shankar to compose the music for *Kabuliwala*. Shankar had already made his mark as a phenomenal music director of feature films with his work in Ray's *Pather Panchali* and *Aparajito* (The Unvanquished, 1956). He visited parts of Afghanistan before the making of *Kabuliwala* and successfully incorporated in the film some of the folk tunes that he collected during his tour.

For the central character of Rahmat, the Afghan trader on the streets of Calcutta, Tapan approached legendary Bengali actor Chhabi Biswas. Biswas had more than a hundred films to his name and commanded a measure of public adulation second to none, not even the romantic stars of the time. He had played a minor role in Tapan's *Upahar*, but Rahmat remains one of his finest performances alongside those in Ray's *Jalsaghar* (The Music Room, 1958), *Devi* (The Goddess, 1960) and *Kanchenjunga* (1962). To Biswas's credit, his Rahmat "remained the epitome of the Kabuliwalas on the streets of Calcutta to generations of film-goers so much so that they were often collectively referred to as 'Rahmat'. The flow of Afghan migrants to Calcutta in the early part of the last century (to mostly trade in dry fruits) has dwindled over the last few decades. However, the endearing bond that develops between an aged Afghan and a little Bengali girl in the film, transcending the barriers of language, caste and creed, appeals to us even today. And the last representatives of the Kabuliwalas in

Calcutta continue to take pride in the personal reference to the iconic character."[3]

Getting Biswas to play an Afghan was not an easy task for Tapan. Primarily because Tapan was relatively new and young as opposed to the seasoned Biswas—less a director's actor and more a follower of his own time-tested mannerisms. In his memoir, *Bioscoper Banke Banke* (A Journey with the Bioscope), Tapan reminisces about how Biswas tried to convince him that he was an authority on the Kabuliwalas. "I earnestly told him: 'Okay, then you must be familiar with the Pashto language as well. I am thinking of keeping some parts of the dialogue in Pashto.' He became a bit concerned: 'Oh, why did you bring Pashto in the dialogues? Who will understand it?' I replied, 'It's fine if people here don't understand it. But this may add to the dimension of acting.' He agreed and confirmed that he would learn it from a Kabuliwala he already knew: 'Leave it to me, the dress, make-up, physical gestures—this is a worthy role after a really long time and I am up for it.' I told him about a flat in Prince Anwar Shah Road where a number of Kabuliwalas stayed together. I actually asked one of them to visit Chhabi-da from time to time."[4]

The interaction with the real-life Kabuliwalas proved futile as Tapan discovered on the first day of the shoot with Biswas: "I was surprised. Who am I seeing before my eyes? Instead of a poor Kabuliwala trading dry fruits on the streets of Calcutta, here is someone who seems to rise up from the tomb of Mohammed Bin Tughlaq, wearing a turban with zari work, an expensive silk dress with zari embroidery accompanied by nagra shoes with golden zari on them. At that time, I was truly an inconsequential director and he was one of the most significant names in

From the family album: A young Tapan with his beloved sister Usharani Ghosh (*Siddhartha Ghosh*)

Tapan with his mother Pramila Sundari Devi (*Sukumar Roy*)

Tapan Sinha and Arundhati Devi on location for a film, 1958 (*Shoma A. Chatterji*)

Tapan Sinha with his old friend, actor Abhi Bhattacharya, 1960 (*Anindya Sinha*)

Members of the film unit of *Kshudhita Pashan* being felicitated by the then Governor of Bihar, Zakir Hussain Khan, after it won the All India Certificate of Merit for Second Best Feature Film, 1961 (*Anindya Sinha*)

Receiving the All India Certificate of Merit for Second Best Feature Film for *Kshudhita Pashan* at the 8th National Film Awards from Vice-President Sarvepalli Radhakrishnan, New Delhi, 31 March 1961 (*Anindya Sinha*)

Explaining a scene to Dilip Kumar and Saira Bano for *Sagina Mahato*, 1967 (*Sukumar Roy*)

Directing Vyjayanthimala in *Hatey Bazarey*, 1967 (Chalachchitra Ajibon, *Ed. Shamik Bandyopadhyay, Dey's Publishing, 2009)*

Hemanta Kumar, Dr Bali, Vyjayanthimala, Tapan Sinha and Ashit Chowdhury, 1967 (*Purnima Dutta*)

Arundhati Devi, Sachin Dev Burman, Tapan Sinha and others during the premiere of *Zindagi Zindagi*, 1972 (*Anindya Sinha*)

Tapan Sinha and others during music rehearsals for *Harmonium*, 1976 (*Anindya Sinha*)

Receiving the Best Children's Film award for *Safed Haathi* from President Neelam Sanjiva Reddy at the 25th National Film Awards, New Delhi, April 1978 (*Anindya Sinha*)

With Arundhati Devi (*Anindya Sinha*)

A family moment: With his actress-director wife Arundhati Devi and son Anindya Sinha (*Anindya Sinha*)

Sharing a light moment with Shatrughan Sinha (*Anindya Sinha*)

In conversation with Waheeda Rehman (*Anindya Sinha*)

With Satyajit Ray (*Anindya Sinha*)

The director's gaze
(*Sukumar Roy*)

With actor Nirmal Kumar
(*Anindya Sinha*)

At work (*Sukumar Roy*)

Explaining a scene to Shabana Azmi in *Ek Doctor Ki Maut*, 1991 (*Sukumar Roy*)

Anindya Sinha recording a song for his father's last film, *Chaar Choritro*, made for TV, 2004 (*Anindya Sinha*)

Bengali cinema. I kept thinking ignorance is bliss. Producer Asit Choudhury visited the set in the afternoon and was quite taken aback by the make-up. This went on for a few days of shooting and then, one day, Asit Choudhury told me about his unhappiness with the make-up. He insisted I forego the shots that had already been done and start afresh with Chhabi-da in proper make-up ... The two of us went up to Chhabi-da and told him that we had to discard the shots done till that time. He was stunned and argued that a poor Kabuliwala might also have some luxury habits. I told him that Rabindranath's Rahmat was not like that. This finally settled the matter. A new set of tattered clothes were tailored for him and the legendary Chhabi Biswas had to accept it though without much joy."[5]

Biswas, however, got his way a number of times during the shoot. He did not allow the make-up person to apply spirit gum to fix his beard and insisted on having theatrical make-up done (this remains in the film). Tapan's memoir mentions a hilarious incident, which reveals how Biswas used to exercise his influence and control on young, new directors. The team was shooting at a locale in Kashmir where the landscape resembled the terrain of Afghanistan. Tapan was not feeling well and wanted to finish work quickly. Chhabi Biswas was supposed to reach the spot after getting his make-up done.

"We were waiting for them. Finally they arrived in a jeep. I could see Rahmat from a distance. But who was the person wearing a suit who alighted from the jeep after Chhabi Biswas? When the group got closer, I was startled. The suited person was Chhabi Biswas himself. Then who was the person with Rahmat's make-up? The moment Chhabi-da came up to me, he praised the location and said, 'This is such an exotic landscape. Will you waste the film by taking my close-up in such a beautiful landscape? That is why I asked your assistant Balai (Sen) to put on the make-up. In a longshot no one will be able to make out the difference.' Needless to say, in the scenes depicting Kabul in *Kabuliwala*, people actually watch Balai Sen instead of Chhabi Biswas!"[6]

*Kabuliwala* became a runaway hit. It placed Tapan in the pantheon of Bengal's (and India's) greatest film-makers. The impact of *Kabuliwala*'s popularity was so strong that Hemen Gupta—whose *Bhuli Nai* (The Unforgotten, 1948), *'42* (1951) and *Anandamath* (The House of Happiness, 1952) were influential films in their own right—opted to make a Hindi version of it in 1961, the birth centenary year of Tagore. However, the Hindi version produced by the legendary Bimal Roy and starring one of Indian cinema's finest actors, Balraj Sahni, could not match the eloquence of Tapan's version. Tapan's *Kabuliwala* not only fared well at the box office in Bengal but also ran for six weeks in Pune in the morning shows.

The film critic of *Jugantar* praised *Kabuliwala* and Tapan: "Tapan Sinha's *Kabuliwala* is not only an excellent characterisation of the Tagore story in Bengali cinema but also a distinguished exception. Director Sinha has successfully portrayed the inherent philosophy of the story. There have been several examples based on successful Bengali literature, but I doubt if we have ever seen any other film which depicts the literary thought of the story so effectively ... Screenplay writer and director Tapan Sinha maintains the basic theme and adds new characters and situations in tandem. In the end, he creates a sensitive experience, which is as sweet as it is sad and lingers for long. With this extrapolation of characters and plot, not only is Tagore's story not degraded, but the essence of this universal theme gets reflected in an even brighter light."[7]

At the 4th National Film Awards, *Kabuliwala* swept the jury off its feet and bagged the President's Gold Medal for the All India Best Feature Film as well as the President's Silver Medal for Best Feature Film in Bengali. But the icing on the cake came from Berlin as Ravi Shankar was awarded the Silver Bear Extraordinary Prize of the Jury for his music in *Kabuliwala*.[8] In his memoir, *Chalachchitra Ajibon* (A Life in Cinema), Tapan remembers the press conference in Berlin that year: "He (Chhabi Biswas) was asked by the international press which actor in world cinema he would like to be compared with. Chhabi-da thundered, 'Only the Barrymores.' He meant not just one but both the Barrymore brothers combined—Lionel and John. He had that much confidence."[9] Tapan had said more than once that *Kabuliwala*'s best features were primarily Tagore's simple yet heart-wrenching story and Biswas's acting. Biswas was excellent and consistent throughout the film, but for Tapan, the best scene was the one in which Rehmat is first introduced to Mini.

Mini reminds Rehmat of his daughter who is almost the same age as Mini and lives in faraway Afghanistan: "It was a double play scene—two frames in one. In parallel shots there was a traversal from the current to the past. Chhabi-da's acting in this particular scene was brilliant. I composed the parallel shot concept by using the stick that Rehmat used to carry all the time. In front of the camera, when he moved the stick from left to right, he had an expression that was exemplary. The way he controlled his eye muscles to convey his feelings was astounding to say the least."[10]

For the role of Mini, Tapan introduced four-year-old Tinku Tagore, the daughter of Gitindranath Thakur, a distant descendant of Rabindranath Tagore. She lived in Asansol near Calcutta. (A few years later, Tinku's elder sister, Sharmila, captured the nation's imagination and went on to become one of the biggest stars of Indian cinema.) Tinku was never expected to 'act' during the shoot; she just behaved like a girl her age. Manju Dey, who was a well-wisher and a constant factor in Tapan's early films, played the role of Mini's mother in the film. She mentored Tinku and cajoled her into taking up the role. Ultimately, Tinku managed to pull off an unbelievably sweet portrayal of Mini.

Despite the awards and accolades that came *Kabuliwala*'s way, there were sharp critiques from two people whom Tapan revered. The first was a phone call from none other than Satyajit Ray who told Tapan: "Being a technician yourself, how come you tolerated such a technically poor film? There is no gain in being such a sober person. Never ever compromise on your work."[11] The second came from Raj Kapoor when *Kabuliwala* was being awarded at Berlin. Kapoor was part of the Indian delegation and Kapoor chided Tapan just like Ray: "How could you make such a technically weak film? Had it been a technically good film, *Kabuliwala* would have bagged the Golden Bear. There wouldn't have been any competition."[12]

On multiple occasions, Tapan had admitted his inability to ensure professional quality of his films because of the compromises he was forced to make. In an interview with Rituparno Ghosh, he confessed: "Bimal Mukhopadhyay was my cameraman. He made a tremendous contribution to my cinema, not only technical but also aesthetic. But there was a drawback in art director Suniti Mitra ... I never wanted to vitiate a friendship because of films. Having worked together for four decades, the unit was almost like a family, there was a deep friendship amongst all. For the sake of the relationship we had with each other, I thought let me compromise on my art a bit."[13] This admission reflects Tapan's humane side and explains the lifelong respect he garnered from his crew members.

Swarup Dutta, who debuted in Tapan's *Aponjon* (My Own People, 1968), was categorical: "There is a prevalent trend in Bengali cinema: the bigger the director's fame, the more he is known as an art film director, the less the remuneration allotted to the cast and the crew. I have seen only in Tapan-da's case that not only did everyone receive what they should in terms of remuneration but more importantly, they received it on time. Very few directors pay attention to this. This makes him an exception."[14]

*Kabuliwala* had another sweet significance in Tapan's life. The Indian delegation at Berlin included Arundhati Mukhopadhyay, a distinguished actress feted for her aristocratic looks and histrionic abilities. She was established as an actress with refined tastes alongside the likes of Suchitra Sen and Sabitri Chatterjee though she had acted in far fewer films than either of them. Tapan talked about one evening at Berlin with typical restraint: "Kurfürstendamm is one of the most famous avenues in Berlin, almost like Chowringhee Road in Calcutta. If you walk a few steps to the north of it, you will find a park. On a long and private evening, Arundhati and I sat on a bench in the park. I requested her to sing a song and she sang Tagore's "Pathe Jete Dekechhile More" (You Beckoned Me on the Way). She won me over with that one song. Soon after, Ms. Arundhati Mukhopadhyay became Mrs. Arundhati Sinha."[15] The couple was a model one in the film fraternity, with both complementing each other and maintaining a dignified natural elegance. Arundhati acted in five of Tapan's films and helped him behind the scenes in the others. Tapan became the sounding board for Arundhati in the five films she directed. Theirs was a family of four—Tapan, Arundhati, their son, Anindya, and a daughter from Arundhati's previous marriage to the director Prabhat Mukhopadhyay.

Tapan went back to Tagore's stories on three more occasions—*Kshudhita Pashan* (1960), *Atithi* (1965) and *Kadambini*, a short film within *Satabdir Kanya* (Daughters of this Century), in 1996. Whereas the first two remain important jewels in Tapan's cinematic oeuvre, the last one was scarcely exhibited and had minimal box-office impact. *Kshudhita Pashan* was a difficult story since it did not have a linear narrative like *Kabuliwala*. With this film too, the Visva-Bharati Music Board demanded a minor clarification, but Tapan rode it out using his previous experience with them. The challenge with *Kshudhita Pashan* was in bringing in the two parallel narratives, one real and contemporary and the other dream-like and imaginary and embedded in a different timeline.

It is worth pointing out that like *Khaniker Atithi* (The Momentary Guest), which was made a year earlier, this film revolves around the romantic bond between the protagonist and the female lead. Both films deal with unrequited romance and the pangs of longing in separation as if stating that it is almost impossible to achieve fruition in a man-woman relationship. In *Kshudhita Pashan*, Tapan skilfully juxtaposed the romance between the past and the present, between a recreated time for which both the protagonist and the audience feel a twinge of nostalgia, and the lived experience of a modern-day commoner. The besotted yet unresolved romance between a female from medieval times and a modern man resurfaced in Tapan's next film, the iconic *Jhinder Bandi*. In it as well, the dummy Sankar Singh's (Uttam Kumar's masterful performance in a double role) love for Rani Kasturi Bai of Jharoa remains unfulfilled. The queen, having lost her heart to a common man, reconciles with her royal constraints in the end. Even in *Jotugriha* (The House of Lacquer, 1964), one of Tapan's best films, the theme of unfulfilled love between the hero and heroine is established with similar empathy and resonance. Interestingly, in all three films, the lovelorn female lead was played by Arundhati Mukhopadhyay.

*Kshudhita Pashan* had prolonged night sequences to create the mystic feeling of light and shade. This automatically made the technical aspect of it more complex. The proper location to portray current times and the medieval dream needed a special *haveli* (mansion) sort of residence. Tapan and producer Hemen Ganguly set out on a tour of western and central India. They even visited Satyendranath Tagore's house in Ahmedabad, where his younger brother Rabindranath Tagore had written *Kshudhita Pashan*. The house was built in the Mughal era and was in a shambles when Tapan visited it. Finally, he found a suitable mansion in Bhopal. However, the Nawab's palace posed a problem—the gigantic pillars and the expansive corridors were likely to cause trouble while filming the night scenes.

A workable solution came from Satyajit Ray with whom Tapan shared a cordial, lifelong relationship: "It was Satyajit Ray who suggested I include Jafri design in the Fatehpuri art installations. At that time, we had a great relationship between film-makers. There was mutual respect and we tried to help each other out … After coming back to Calcutta, I met him one day at New Theatres Studio. He was using the editing room on one of the Studio floors regularly to work on his own film. I told him about the difficulty that I would face if I shot the night sequences at the location itself. He commented, 'That will be almost impossible to shoot. Why don't you try out the option of miniature sets as they do in the West?' I then instructed my art director Suniti Mitra to plan for a set typical of the Nawab's palace, but to make it less theatrical than what one normally finds in Bengali films. The very next day, Satyajit-babu met me and handed over a sketch that he had done based on our conversation! The sketch had arches and pillars … My problem was solved instantly. I handed it over to Suniti and instructed him to build a set exactly in line with Satyajit-babu's drawings."[16]

Tapan chose Radhamohan Bhattacharjee and Chhabi Biswas to play two important supporting roles in the film. For the female lead (an Arab girl stolen from the Arabian deserts), Tapan cast Arundhati Mukhopadhyay who exuded natural charm, elegance and an alluringly distanced air of surrealism. The professional and personal bond between Arundhati and Tapan enriched their creative pursuits and provided both with aesthetic sustenance in the years to come. For the role of the young protagonist, Tapan zoomed in on Soumitra Chatterjee who had two films, Ray's *Apur Sansar* (The World of Apu, 1959) and *Devi* (Goddess, 1960) to his credit. Tapan states in his memoir, *Amar Jiban, Amar Chhabi* (My Life, My Films): "What fantastic preparations Soumitra went through for the role. A lot of hard work … Every morning he would train in horse riding. I decided to cast him right after watching *Apur Sansar*. So I asked Satyajit-babu, 'I am thinking of casting Soumitra. Does he come to shoots on time, is he sincere?' Satyajit-babu readily confirmed, 'You can cast Soumitra without any hesitation. He listens to directors and is very serious about his work' … After shooting for a couple of days, I could make out that Soumitra was perfect."[17]

After the musical success of *Kabuliwala* courtesy Ravi Shankar, Tapan went on to work with Ali Akbar Khan, another master of Indian classical music. Both Hindi and Bengali cinema boasted of stalwart music composers at that time—S.D. Burman, Hemanta Mukhopadhyay, Naushad, Madan Mohan, Salil Choudhury, Shankar-Jaikishen and O.P. Nayyar. The list was long and illustrious. There was no dearth of soulful musical tunes although the focus was more on songs rather than just background scores. Ali Akbar Khan had just started off as a music composer in the Bombay film industry when he came on board to work on the music of *Kshudhita Pashan*: "*Kshudhita Pashan* was my musical tribute to Rabindranath Tagore. The director of the film was Tapan Sinha. Baba (Allauddin Khan) was made to agree to watch the film after a lot of coaxing. I had already started as a music director in Bombay by then which made Baba immensely angry with me. He even thought of disowning me due to this. With a lot of reluctance, Baba went to watch the film and took a side seat so that he could leave the hall whenever he felt like it. By God's grace, he liked my music in *Kshudhita Pashan* so much that he gave me permission to continue as a music composer in films."[18]

The film's music turned out to be phenomenal with a rare fusion of Rabindra Sangeet and Indian classical music sung by Ustad Amir Khan, one of the most influential figures of Indian classical music. Tapan explains in his memoir how bemused he became when he encountered the genius of Ali Akbar. "I told him that I was thinking of a basic musical score with Raga Bageshree Kanada. Ali-da thought for a moment and then played five or six variations of Bageshree's *mukhda* (start of an Indian classical musical piece). He said, 'Let me know which one amongst these you like, I will make music with it.' I was utterly confused since all of them were excellent. Finally we zeroed in on the one which was closest to Rabindranath's "Je Rate Mor Duarguli Bhanglo Jhore" (On the Night When the Storm Breaks Down My Door)."[19]

*Kshudhita Pashan* was released on 6 May 1960, two days before the ninety-ninth birth anniversary of Rabindranath Tagore. It became a box-office hit running to houseful shows for months till the Durga Puja at the end of September. At the 8th National Film Awards in 1961, it bagged the All India Certificate of Merit. Critics welcomed it with open arms as well. The film critic of *Anandabazar Patrika* commented: "Is it possible to make a successful film out of a work of literary genius like *Kshudhita Pashan*? Can an artistically brilliant film become popular with the general audience at the same time? Today, we have an answer to both these questions. Mr. Sinha has gifted us with his best film till date. The unadulterated exuberance of the general film-goer makes his attempt a resounding success ... The director never allows the film to digress from its natural rhythm. The uniqueness of natural expression in Tapan Sinha's style is more mature in this film."[20]

The film critic of the leading daily, *Jugantar*, went further: "It will not be unjust to say that *Kshudhita Pashan* is entirely a work of art of Tapan Sinha. The viewer will understand this while watching the film. The director has expressed a rare balance in this film—mastery over the art of theatrics and a sensitive restraint in portrayal. Along with his directorial efficiency, one must not overlook his proficiency in scriptwriting as well."[21]

While analysing the uniqueness and brilliance of *Kshudhita Pashan* after more than five decades of its release, noted scholar Amrit Sen comments: "In drawing upon the incarnation of an earlier birth and a historical romance that drew upon the debauchery and cruelty of a Mughal ruler, Sinha was already falling back within the comfortable confines of popular expectations that were sure to appeal to the regular Bengali film-goer. Therefore, Sinha needed the relative simplicity and financial safety to create a period piece embellished with the classical music of Ali Akbar Khan, without any encroachment of sceptical possibility. One notes that Sinha was keenly sensitive to the aptness of this particular story for the various possibilities of cinematic narrative ... Sinha rearranges the narrative into a more linear plot while foregrounding the visual aspect of light and shade to create an ambience of fear and mystery within which all scepticism could dissolve into an aesthetic enjoyment of the supernatural.

"The technical innovations of the film need to be appreciated. The innovative set designs, the use of silence, the use of the mirror and the slow flying away of the hat, attempt a conjunction of the two temporal zones that the film inhabits. Sinha provides a visual treat in combining music, setting and location to convey and transform *Kshudhita Pashan* into a tale of fascination and supernatural power ... The making of the film and the responses to it also throws light on the myriad expectations of the Bengali *bhadralok* (prosperous, well-educated social class) at this point in history. Faced with the turbulence of the post-Partition era, Sinha's film offered a less complicated, bourgeoisie Rabindranath Tagore in whose narrative the audience could retire for an interval of two hours. Would the exotic locations and costumes, the music of an era that had passed by, create an illusion of a withdrawal of reality? Or was the theme of forced separation from one's location, and the pain and trauma caused by it, a viable shelter for a Bengali audience struggling with the realities of Partition? Would the mode of the romance have been an interlude from the urgent questions about contemporary existence?"[22]

For Tapan, the biggest satisfaction came from taking Rabindranath Tagore to the masses, a challenge which he had accepted at the time of *Kabuliwala*. It is not an exaggeration to say that few directors could make a film on a Tagore story as acceptable to the audience as Tapan. Tapan's three films on Tagore masterpieces remains immensely popular, loved even now and referenced in every critical discussion about the cinematic adaptation of Tagore's stories. Tapan's nephew Siddhartha Kumar Ghosh lists one incident that exemplifies Tapan's role as a rare director who could bridge the divide between art and popular culture: "Once, his mother Pramila Devi was passing by Rupabani Theatres in a taxi when the driver pointed at the poster of *Kshudhita Pashan* and said, 'Ma, have you watched this film? I have watched it four times.' A minor incident but it goes on to reveal the popularity his films could garner at that time."[23]

In an interview with film-maker Raja Sen for the documentary, *Film-maker's Film-making*, centred on Tapan, the film-maker talked about a very important aspect of his career. He hinted at the reason behind his choice of themes and the underlying philosophy of his message: "*Atithi* had a spirit of freedom which was excellently depicted by Tagore in a very small space. This film brought a change in me and I henceforth decided to depict and worship the freedom of man. And gradually, all the windows of my room opened so that I didn't get any chance to look through only one window. I had a global perspective to depict a 'man' as a 'man'. He has to fight his own battle and win and be an example to others. It doesn't matter whether he is literate or illiterate, whether he is handicapped or healthy; it is his life which matters in the end."[24]

Siddhartha Kumar Ghosh remembers another interesting anecdote: "While talking to my father, I discovered that when he was planning with my maternal grandfather (who was in Murshidabad) to bring Tapan to Bhagalpur, the latter was an innocent child running around the *thakur dalan* (part of a Bengali home reserved for performing *puja*) with a flute in hand, sporting a *dhoti* (traditional men's garment wrapped around the lower part of the body). Playing the flute became his passion during the later years of his life. I feel Tarapada of *Atithi* was born right there."

In *Atithi*, Tapan introduced two newcomers in the roles of Tarapada (Partha Mukhopadhyay) and Charu (Basabi Bandopadhyay), daughter of the legendary actor Bhanu Bandopadhyay. Mukhopadhyay was selected from a group of more than 200 adolescent boys. His fair complexion and soulful, innocent eyes inspired Tapan to cast him. For Tapan, *Atithi* was a very important film because it dealt with the unrelenting human urge to break free of the barriers life imposes on individuals. This theme of a wandering individual, uncomfortable with the constraints of a stable life was also made popular by the box-office hit, *Palatak* (The Fugitive, 1963), directed by the noted Bengali film-maker, Tarun Majumdar. The coming of age of the female character, Charu, has many similarities with another film based on a Tagore story, *Samapti* (The Ending, 1961), directed by Satyajit Ray.

Ray provided a piece of valuable input to Tapan: "I (Tapan) came to know that *Atithi* was selected for the Venice Film Festival. Mr. Ray called me up: 'Listen, for the Venice competition, end the film with the shot where we find Tarapada jumping in the water amongst hundreds of boats ... Also, why did you use Tagore's songs for the background score? That was okay for the Calcutta audience but no foreigner will understand its true spirit. Why didn't you compose the music yourself?' I followed Mr. Ray's suggestion and ended the film there. The results were good, I must admit."[25] The film was appreciated in Venice. Back home in India, it won the All India Certificate of Merit for the Second Best Feature Film.

Critics showered lavish praise on the film. The film critic of *Anandabazar Patrika* wrote: "There is no dearth of controversies regarding the cinematic adaptation of a successful work of literature. Whether the film will follow the source, and how much liberty a film-maker can take are pertinent questions. Even serious critics are raising doubts as to whether cinema should be based on literature or not ... Satyajit Ray has already proved with his *Charulata* (The Lonely Wife, 1964) that a masterpiece can be created even if you partially deviate from the original text. Today, we realise that a quality film can also be produced if one follows the written text to the fullest...Tapan Sinha had embarked upon a difficult journey in transcreating the Tagore story. Today we can say without doubt that he has passed this test with flying colours."[26]

Siddhartha Kumar Ghosh says that when acting legend Dilip Kumar expressed the desire to watch *Atithi*, a special screening was arranged for him in Calcutta: "I am told that he was so spellbound that he stayed quiet for a couple of minutes and then said, 'Tapan, I was like Tarapada in my childhood.' *Atithi* is a powerful film that lets us experience a blissful state of existence and makes us all want to be part of it."

The adventurer in Tapan took two significant steps with *Atithi*. This was his first venture without any stars—his actors were amateurs or new to cinema. More importantly, this was the first film in which Tapan worked as the music director as well. From then on, he went on to don the hat of music director for his Bengali films. The lyrical temper of *Atithi* can be attributed partially to Tagore—not just the story but also the songs. Tapan's upbringing in which music played a substantial part also helped immensely. In *Jhinder Bandi*, Ali Akbar Khan composed a medley of ragas as a background to the prince's drinking spree. It became very popular and beautifully portrayed the character's profligacy in a creative, musical register. In the penultimate scenes of *Atithi*, Tapan used an unusual musical medley that fused Bengali folk songs with the classical. Tarapada loses his 'self' in a milieu, a carnival that celebrates Nature and the joy of freedom in his otherwise confined and adventure-less life.

The medley conveyed Tarapada's inner turmoil, the hesitation before he set himself free and left the zamindar's palatial home and the earthly comforts he enjoyed there. Tagore ended the story with Tarapada merging with Nature from where he originated. Tapan heightened the effect by making Tarapada mix with a crowd at a fair. In doing so, he made the audience aware that Tarapada was as much an incarnation of Tagore on paper as he was that of Tapan onscreen.

## REFERENCES

[1] Tapan Sinha, *Chalachchitra Ajibon*, Ed: Shamik Bandopadhyay, Dey's Publishing, 2009, p. 393 [Translation by the author]

[2] Ibid., pp. 393–394 [Translation by the author]

[3] Amitava Nag, 'Chhabi Biswas–Inimitable and Indomitable', *Silhouette*, 12 July 2015, https://learningandcreativity.com/silhouette/chhabi-biswas/ accessed on 15 March 2018

[4] Tapan Sinha, *Chalachchitra Ajibon*, Ed: Shamik Bandopadhyay, Dey's Publishing, 2009, p. 21 [Translation by the author]

[5] Ibid., pp. 21–22 [Translation by the author]

[6] Ibid., pp. 22–23 [Translation by the author]

[7] Tapan Sinha, *Aamar Jiban Aamar Chhabi, Vol. I*, Compiled by: Asishtoru Mukhopadhyay, Abhijato Publishing, May 1998, p. 47 [Translation by the author]

[8] Prizes & Honours 1957, Berlin Film Festival, https://www.berlinale.de/en/archiv/jahresarchive/1957/03_preistr_ger_1957/03_Preistraeger_1957.html accessed on 15 March 2018

[9] Tapan Sinha, *Chalachchitra Ajibon*, Ed: Shamik Bandopadhyay, Dey's Publishing, 2009, p. 22 [Translation by the author]

[10] Tapan Sinha, *Aamar Jiban Aamar Chhabi, Vol. I*, Compiled by: Asishtoru Mukhopadhyay, Abhijato Publishing, May 1998, p. 47 [Translation by the author]

[11] Ibid., p. 49

[12] Ibid., p. 50

[13] Tapan Sinha, *Chalachchitra Ajibon*, Ed: Shamik Bandopadhyay, Dey's Publishing, 2009, p. 361 [Translation by the author]

[14] Swarup Dutta, 'A Distinguished Exception', *Tapan Sinha Special Issue–Chitravas*, Vol. 38 (No. 1 to 4), January–December 2003, p. 94 [Translation by the author]

[15] Tapan Sinha, *Chalachchitra Ajibon*, Ed: Shamik Bandopadhyay, Dey's Publishing, 2009, p. 91 [Translation by the author]

[16] Tapan Sinha, *Aamar Jiban Aamar Chhabi, Vol. I*, Compiled by: Asishtoru Mukhopadhyay, Abhijato Publishing, May 1998, p. 72 [Translation by the author]

[17] Ibid., p. 81

[18] Nandan Mitra, *Tapan Sinha-r Film-making*, Chalachitra o Sanskriti Charcha Kendra, January 2015, p. 134 [Excerpt from Ustad Ali Akbar Khan's autobiography, *Aapnar Sebay* [Translation by the author]

[19] Tapan Sinha, *Aamar Jiban Aamar Chhabi, Vol. I*, Compiled by: Asishtoru Mukhopadhyay, Abhijato Publishing, May 1998, p. 73 [Translation by the author]

[20] Ibid., pp. 74, 76

[21] Ibid., p. 77

[22] Amrit Sen, 'Modes of Storytelling: Tapan Sinha's *Kshudhita Pashan*', *Silhouette,* 10 November 2012, https://learningandcreativity.com/silhouette/modes-of-storytelling-tapan-sinhas-kshudita-pashan-1961/ accessed on 15 March 2018

[23] Siddhartha Kumar Ghosh, 'Chalachchitre Chandomoy Jogoter Srosta–Tapan Sinha', *Tapan Sinha Special Issue–Chitravas*, Vol. 38 No. 1–4), January–December 2003, p. 43 [Translation by the author]

[24] Documentary film on Tapan Sinha, *Film-maker's Film-making*, by Raja Sen

[25] Tapan Sinha, *Chalachchitra Ajibon*, Ed: Shamik Bandopadhyay, Dey's Publishing, 2009, p. 88 [Translation by the author]

[26] Tapan Sinha, *Aamar Jiban Aamar Chhabi, Vol. I*, Compiled by: Asishtoru Mukhopadhyay, Abhijato Publishing, May 1998, pp. 115–116 [Translation by the author]

তারাশঙ্করের
হাঁসুলী বাঁকের
উপকথা

# The Rest of the Literary Phase

In multiple interviews, Tapan mentioned his preference for literature when it came to sourcing the content of his films. In this regard, he is closer to Satyajit Ray than to Mrinal Sen or Ritwik Ghatak. Apart from a few exceptions including Tarashankar Bandopadhyay's *Hanshuli Banker Upakatha* (Folk Tales of the River Bend, 1962), Tapan felt more comfortable working on short stories instead of novels. Bengali literature has a rich repertoire of short stories, made popular by Rabindranath Tagore and then enriched by most of the prominent prose writers of the language. These writers hailed from all over Bengal, not just the city of Calcutta. Hence the stories reflected the lives of diverse socio-economic strata. This expansive spectrum lent Tapan's films an enviable variety which few Indian film-makers could dream of achieving.

From his first film *Ankush*, Tapan followed the practice of relying on literary texts and continued to do so for the next decade. Though he deviated from this for a film or two, the first 15 years of his career can be safely called his literary phase. During this time, Tapan chose classical stories that were highly literary. Ray also followed a similar trajectory by delving into the works of the greats of Bengali literature from his first film, *Pather Panchali* up to *Aranyer Din Ratri* (Days and Nights in the Forest) in 1970. In the sixties and seventies, Tapan and Ray were on the lookout for work revolving around more contemporary subjects—either written by themselves or by authors of their time, a period marred and marked by the Naxalite movement. On the contrary, Mrinal Sen had already focused on the angst of the urban youth with films like *Pratinidhi* (The Representative, 1964) and *Akash Kusum* (Up in the Clouds, 1965) in the early to mid-sixties.

In 1958, still fresh from the international success of *Kabuliwala*, Tapan made two feature films—*Louhakapat* and *Kalamati* (Black Soil, 1958). In *Kabuliwala*, the protagonist was not a Bengali middle-class educated youth, something he continued to stick with in both *Louhakapat* and *Kalamati*. After the lyricism of Tagore's stories, Tapan turned to a more rooted reality—the life of prisoners in jail. Charu Chandra Chakrabarti, who wrote under the pseudonym Jarasandha, was a jailor who had penned some of the classics of Bengali literature based on his real-life experiences. His story, *Tamasi* (Darkness), gained popularity after Bimal Roy made *Bandini* (The Imprisoned) in 1963, a landmark Hindi film based on *Tamasi*. *Louhakapat,* Jarasandha's first novel, was published as a series in the leading Bengali literary magazine, *Desh*. Tapan's decision to make a film on the lives of prisoners was a unique pioneering attempt. He shot the film within the premises of the Alipore Jail in Calcutta, lending an extra bit of legitimacy to the movie's realistic setting. Tapan picked Bimal Mukhopadhyay as his cinematographer. Though Tapan went back to his cinematographer friend Anil Bandopadhyay for his next two films, it was his association with Mukhopadhyay that lasted the longest in his film-making career.

*Louhakapat* bagged the Certificate of Merit for Second Best Feature Film in the Regional Awards (Bengali) category and was a box-office hit. The film's success and the critical acclaim it garnered gave Tapan the confidence to take more risks with his literary sources. Not only did he try out new narratives that were hitherto unseen on the Indian screen but he also experimented with stories by new and lesser-known writers. For example, his next film, *Kalamati*, was adapted from a short story by the then emerging Bengali writer, Ramapada Chaudhuri. The story revolved round a crèche for babies at a colliery. To create an authentic feel, Tapan made sure he did his homework extensively. Before writing the script, he went to the colliery of Raniganj Coalfield, the first of its kind in India. He descended to the base of the coalmine to observe the work done there. While shooting the film, he would take the camera deep into the mine to capture the look and feel of the interior. Obviously, this was technically challenging and physically hazardous for people who were not accustomed to working in coalmines.

Tapan's friend, Anil Bandopadhyay, who had encouraged him to become a director from early on, was the cinematographer of *Kalamati*. His assistant, Sankar Guha, described the harsh rigour of the shoot: "We used to leave for work at 6 in the morning. We worked both on the ground and also deep in the mine. Underground, we had to carry lights of 110 volts by hand ... At times the camera was put on a stand, but mostly it was handheld. It was very cold at the deepest point, but the place where coal extraction was being done was extremely hot. We used to keep sliced lemons in our mouths. No doubt it was a very adventurous and important work at that time."[1]

Bandopadhyay did remarkably well at adjusting the exposure of the camera to counter the weak light inside the tunnels in the mine. In *Kalamati*, the lead character, Anupama, is an educated, enlightened woman who runs the crèche. Tapan cast Arundhati Mukhopadhyay as Anupama. This was her first appearance in a Tapan Sinha film.

Filming *Kalamati* was a major challenge for Tapan because of the sheer size of the project—the outdoor unit comprised nearly a hundred artists, technicians and crew. The outdoor shoot happened at the Sanctoria colliery. The film's music was composed by Ravi Shankar (the last time the maestro worked with Tapan). *Anandabazar Patrika's* film critic mentioned an extremely important aspect: "Along with the different kinds of work that is done in a coalmine, the director also introduces us to the life of coal labourers. In fact, there has been no other film in Indian cinema till date with such a bona fide depiction of a colliery. In this light, *Kalamati* is a significantly successful creation."[2]

Till 1970, starting from his debut *Ankush* in 1954 to *Sagina Mahato*, Tapan wrote the stories for only two of his 18 films: *Galpa Holeo Satyi* (A True Story, 1966) and *Khaniker Atithi*. In a sense, this shows his commitment towards literary works (his sources) by established authors. *Galpa Holeo Satyi* which was later 'remade' in Hindi by Hrishikesh Mukherjee as *Bawarchi* (The Chef, 1972), featured Tapan's name in the title cards as the writer. Tapan had made *Khaniker Atithi* in 1959 based on his own story, but he used the fictional name of Nirmal Kumar Sengupta for this film. Chances are that he arrived at this name after he cast Nirmal Kumar as the hero of *Khaniker Atithi*.

The protagonist of *Khaniker Atithi*, Bimal, is a doctor who works at a rural hospital in West Bengal. This was Tapan's first film with a doctor as the central character. He went on to make quite a few after this with the idealistic, noble and benevolent doctor as the protagonist. Tapan's personal belief in an individual's struggle and conflicts, and his rise from the ashes to become a larger-than-life figure for the greater good, are depicted through the 'doctor character' in several of his films like *Arohi* (Ascent, 1965), *Hatey Bazarey* (The Marketplace, 1967), *Ek Doctor Ki Maut* (The Death of a Doctor, *1991*), *Zindagi Zindagi* (Life Life, 1972) and *Wheel Chair* (1994).

*Khaniker Atithi* does not end on a happy note as Bimal loses the woman he loves, Mita, early on (shown primarily in flashbacks), gets her back when she returns to him as a widow with a son who is unwell, and then leaves him again when her son recovers. The lyricism of the film along with the low-key, subtle performances of Nirmal Kumar and Ruma Guha Thakurta make for enriching viewing though. *Khaniker Atithi* was one of Tapan's favourite films: "The audience accepted it gladly ... I liked the film because I could portray the poetic essence of it. The origin of this lyricism is undoubtedly Tagore ... Hemanta Mukhopadhyay (the music director of the film) told me: 'This film is nothing but poetry. I will use Rabindra Sangeet for its background score.' He used the Tagore song "Pathe Jete Jete Dekechhile More" (You Have Called My Name As You Travelled)."[3]

*Khaniker Atithi* was 'remade' by Tapan himself in 1972 as *Zindagi Zindagi* with Sunil Dutt and Waheeda Rehman in the lead. The Hindi version lacked the elegance of the

Bengali film primarily because Tapan had to introduce a number of subplots to satisfy the pan-Hindi audience. He was less sure about this audience and its preferences. Most importantly, he had to compromise on the film's ending by making it a happy one with the union of Mita and Bimal.

On 6 May 1960, Tapan's *Kshudhita Pashan* was released. In the same year, Tapan and Arundhati's only son, Anindya, was born on 1 October. Growing up in such a culturally rich ambience inculcated the necessary values in Anindya. He, however, chose to pursue a career in science while living a life steeped in music and literature. An alumnus of the prestigious Presidency College, Kolkata, and the Tata Institute of Fundamental Research, Bombay, Anindya is a professor at the National Institute of Advanced Studies under the aegis of the Indian Institute of Science, Bengaluru.

The real-life bond between Tapan and Arundhati was equally fertile onscreen as they embarked on Tapan's next project, *Jhinder Bandi*. It remains a magnum opus for Tapan as well as Bengali cinema for many reasons—a fairytale of epic proportions, a crime thriller with several outdoor settings, starring Soumitra Chatterjee and Uttam Kumar together for the first time. Though Tapan never explicitly stated that it was his personal favourite, the film exceeded his expectations. Soumitra Chatterjee's portrayal of the rakish villain, Mayurbahan, is the epitome of histrionic expression and one of the best performances of his legendary career of six decades. The film is based on Saradindu Bandopadhyay's novel of the same name, which is a faithful adaptation of Anthony Hope's popular novel, *The Prisoner of Zenda*. In Hollywood, the novel was made into a film twice—once in 1937 starring Ronald Colman in a double role and Douglas Fairbanks Jr. as the villain, and again in 1952 with Stewart

Granger and James Mason essaying the central characters of the king and the villain respectively.

Tapan effectively used the Hollywood influence by dressing his actors in Western outfits, but he also retained some prominent features of the traditional Indian royal dress including the turban. Both Soumitra Chatterjee and Uttam Kumar were trained to ride horses and learn fencing from Masey Taylor who had participated in the Olympics. Soumitra who had debuted two years ago in Ray's *Apur Sansar* was considered to be adept at playing the educated Tagorean middle-class Bengali. Casting him in his seventh film as a villain was indeed a phenomenal experiment. Tapan said: "Many people were surprised when I cast Soumitra as Mayurbahan in *Jhinder Bandi.* But I was confident about him playing the part because he is a highly skilled actor, one who, I felt, was eminently capable of variations in acting and should not be limited to playing romantic roles only. In Western films, the best actors try to break away from the mould when possible. Why can't we do the same here? Any great actor needs to be versatile and try a range of roles.

"When I called Soumitra and told him about my plan, he readily agreed to play Mayurbahan. During our discussion, I told him that there was a basic difference between Mayurbahan and the character he had played in my earlier film, *Kshudhita Pashan.* He would have to cultivate an entirely different style of walking, dialogue delivery, etc. Mayurbahan had to be good at fencing, horse riding. His is a devil-may-care personality ready to take any risk: intelligent but a bit of a ruffian. It was (considering the roles he had played so far) a total breakaway, that of the typical baddie. Soumitra acted brilliantly as Mayurbahan, and that is universally acknowledged now."[4]

Veteran actor Dhritiman Chaterji described Soumitra's portrayal as a landmark in Indian cinema. "So, in 1961, here was this twenty-six-year-old actor being cast against a veteran, a star, a legend who was more than 80 films old, a casting coup if ever there was one ... It would not be overstating it to say that, with Mayurbahan, the Bengali audience sat up and took notice of this young actor and all sorts of debates began about who was the superior actor in *Jhinder Bandi*, who was to be the face of Bengali cinema and so on ... Even though the film was set in some unspecified feudal time, it was contemporary in terms of the core idea and realistic in its execution. And the same realism pervaded Soumitra's portrayal of Mayurbahan. It overflowed with youthful vigour, resisted the conventional villain image and cleverly counterpointed the regality of Uttam Kumar and the gravity of Radhamohan Bhattacharjee."[5]

Ali Akbar Khan who composed the music for *Kshudhita Pashan* worked on *Jhinder Bandi* as well. Tapan used music to great effect to portray the debauched character of Prince Sankar Singh, a man with many vices. The one silver lining in his character was his love for Indian classical music. Tapan had Ali Akbar Khan compose a medley of ragas, one flowing into the next, and he used it as the background score in the scene where Sankar Singh goes on a drinking spree. The effect was evocative, leaving the audience hungry for more of the composition. Later, while composing the music for *Atithi*, Tapan followed the same strategy in the climactic scene where Tarapada loses himself in the crowd.

After telling a story set in the chilly terrain of Rajasthan in *Jhinder Bandi*, Tapan moved on to rugged rural Bengal in *Hanshuli Banker Upakatha* the following year. Based on a novel by Tarashankar Bandopadhyay, this film deals with a set of subalterns who are marginalised in rural Bengali society. Tapan, unlike Ghatak, had never dealt with the theme of the Partition of Bengal in a direct way. In a sense, *Hanshuli Banker Upakatha* was Tapan's way of addressing the issue of displacement and the crises and miseries of the unfortunate refugees. Tapan had elaborate sessions with the novelist himself who took him on a tour of the Birbhum district of West Bengal so he could better understand the essence of the story. This detailed recce opened new windows in Tapan's mind and he decided to use the actual, abandoned houses of the people whom Tarashankar had observed and turned into characters for his novel. Tarashankar wrote the songs for the film as well.

The film's sensitivity was enhanced by a melodious musical score and extremely competent camerawork by the cinematographer, Bimal Mukhopadhyay. The film opens with a compelling, uninterrupted tracking shot over a minute long. Noted cinematographer Kamal Nayek, who worked with Tapan much later in *Atanka* (Fear, 1986), recalls: "To bring in that distinct visual pattern of the opening scene with the palanquin, the way a discarded train line was used for a 300–400-metre-long tracking shot was unthinkable at that time. There were two palanquins. They were moving in a serpentine way. At times, the levels were different as well, based on the unevenness of the terrain. At times, one of them could be hidden behind a bunch of trees, at times, the camera panned to capture the other—these visual variations in composition were worth picking up even for a professional cinematographer. In parallel, there was a song which the bearers were singing. That too was alternately used between the first and the second palanquin. As a result, the entire scene is never monotonous."[6]

A saga of such enormous proportions meant that the shooting unit comprised over a hundred people. Tapan did put in a lot of hard work, shooting for eight to ten months at a stretch at different locations and capturing the realistic effect of the changing seasons. Unfortunately, the film did not fare well at the box office though it was critically acclaimed. The film critic of the leading Bengali daily, *Anandabazar Patrika,* commented: "*Hanshuli Banker Upakatha* raises hopes in our minds about new Bengali cinema. It even helps us forget the pain we experience as we witness the crisis of contemporary Bengali cinema. Where it is possible to make such a film, can there be a crisis? Or, even if it is possible, how long can the crisis linger?"[7]

Given his interest in literature as a source for his films, Tapan Sinha kept looking for exciting young authors with new stories to tell. Samaresh Basu, who wrote under the pen name Kalkut, was one such writer who observed life closely through his works. Kalkut's *Amrita Kumbher Sandhane* (The Quest for the Pitcher of Nectar), set at the holy Kumbh mela, is an unsentimental record of the confluence of Hindus from different parts of the country there. Tapan had eyed *Amrita Kumbher Sandhane* for a long time. Unfortunately, he did not get a chance to adapt the novel into a film since the film rights were sold to Bimal Roy. Roy did not make the film, and much later, actor Dilip Roy (who acted as Karali in *Hanshuli Banker Upakatha*), brought the novel to the screen. Kalkut suggested Tapan read another novel of his with a similar setting—*Nirjan Saikate* (The Desolate Beach). Tapan liked the story. In late 1962, he started filming *Nirjan Saikate* at the seaside at Puri.

The film revolved around four widows and their young niece who go to Puri on a pilgrimage and a vacation. The narrative was simple and linear. The characters of the four widows were endearing and the actresses did a good job of essaying them. Tapan says in his memoir: "Chhaya Devi, Renuka Roy, Bharati Devi and Ruma Guha Thakurta put in a lot of effort into their acting. They were rewarded soon—jointly awarded the Best Actress Award in the International Film Festival of India in 1963. I don't know if there is a similar feat where four actresses bagged the award together for the same film. In that way, it is a special award in my life as well."[8] The Best Actress Award was actually shared between five people—the four actresses and Sharmila Tagore who played their niece. This was Tagore's only film with Tapan. It was made before she migrated to Bombay to become one of Hindi cinema's most popular heroines.

Chhaya Devi, who appeared in many of Tapan's films, was at her sublime best in *Nirjan Saikate*. Tapan held her in high regard and cast her in film after film: "To me, Chhaya Devi was the greatest actress of Bengali cinema of all time ... I have observed with awe how she evolved in her acting. Acting as a vocation changes with time and she is always up-to-date. Otherwise she wouldn't stand out amongst the other great actors. This is why in my mind I have a special and distinct space for her as an actor."[9]

From the seashore to the heart of a ruthless metropolis, Tapan shifted his focus from four widows and a jilted lover to the heart of a marriage conundrum next. *Jotugriha* (1964) remains one of Tapan's most flawless films. It is based on a short story by Subodh Ghosh who was popular with film-makers of the time including Bimal Roy (*Sujata*, 1959,

Hindi), Ritwik Ghatak (*Ajantrik,* The Pathetic Fallacy, 1958, Bengali), Basu Chatterjee (*Chitchor,* The Heart Stealer, 1976, Hindi) and Tarun Majumdar (*Thagini,* The Lady Thug, 1974, Bengali). Years later, Gulzar made *Ijaazat* (Permission, 1988, Hindi) based on the same story though his version was distinctly different from Sinha's.

From the mid-fifties to the end of the next decade, Tapan churned out roughly one film per year. In his entire career, he only cast Uttam Kumar, the matinee idol and biggest Bengali star till date, thrice and that too without his two leading ladies—Suchitra Sen and Supriya Devi. It is to Tapan's credit that in spite of this, his films, unlike those of other stalwarts of the time, were successes at the box office and also festival favourites.

For *Jotugriha*, it was Uttam Kumar who approached Tapan as a producer. Kumar had produced films in collaboration with others and had films like *Harano Sur* (The Lost Melody, 1957) and *Saptapadi* (Seven Steps, 1961) under the banner of Alochhaya Productions Private Limited to his credit. In 1962, he launched his own production company—Uttam Kumar Films Private Limited. Tapan recalled: "Uttam came to my house one day in the morning and told me, 'I have started a production house. Asit Choudhury is also there with me. Will you make a film for us?' I asked him, 'What subject do you want to do?' Uttam replied, 'It's up to you. You will take up whatever subject you wish to. If you think that I will not fit any of the characters, you need not cast me.' I thought that it will not be proper not to cast Uttam in his own home production. I was interested in working on Subodh Ghosh's *Jotugriha* and I told him to read the story. Uttam liked the story as well … Uttam and Arundhati both had to convey a lot silently in this film.

This is very tough. Uttam was adept at all sorts of acting. He was magnificent in *Jotugriha* also."[10]

Though he was all praise for Kumar and Arundhati, Tapan was self-critical: "I couldn't do justice to the outdoor scenes. The shooting was done in the steamer-ghat of Sahebganj. I was upset and lost my mental cool due to the immense crowd during the shooting. In the last scene the concept of 'The night stars lie deep in the light of the day' was not tactfully done. I should have been more restrained."[11]

Peering into the heart of the upwardly mobile, ambitious Bengali middle class of the sixties, Tapan brought the issues of marital discord and infertility into his film. As a counterpoint of Satadal and Madhuri (played by Kumar and Arundhati), he introduces us to two other families—that of Nikhilesh and Sushama who are in the same strata as Satadal's and that of Supriyo and his wife who are definitely at a lower rung. Nikhilesh and Sushama share a loveless, deceitful relationship. They fight endlessly and in front of their young child, reminding us of Francois Truffaut's poignantly painful *400 Blows*. On the other hand, Supriyo and his wife lead an apparently ideal conjugal life. With great affection, Tapan etched the characters of Satadal and Madhuri who refrain from slandering each other. The film went on to bag the Certificate of Merit for the Third Best Feature Film at the 11th National Film Awards. *Jotugriha* was Tapan's attempt at reflecting urban middle-class life, a theme he would return to predominantly in the seventies and eighties when he chose topical subjects and used cinema as a medium of social reflection.

At the height of his creative surge, Tapan started work on his next film barely months after *Jotugriha*. This one was based on *Arjun Mandal*, a short story by Banaphool.

Banaphool (a doctor by profession) hailed from Bhagalpur where Tapan had grown up. He had a natural affinity towards the writer. *Arohi*, Tapan's thirteenth film in ten years since *Ankush*, lauds the individual's triumph against all odds, a philosophy to which Tapan adhered throughout his life. The film won the President's Silver Medal for Best Feature Film (Bengali) at the 12th National Film Awards, the All India Certificate of Merit for the Best Story Writer, the Interfilm Award at the 1965 Locarno Film Festival[12] and a Certificate of Merit at the London Film Festival.[13]

Tapan had a clear purpose when he set out to make *Arohi*: "Satyajit Ray once said, 'In order to make a good film, the first task is to educate the audience.' I made the film inspired by what Ray said."[14] *Arohi* was indeed an inspirational film that made the audience dream big, think big. Kali Bandopadhyay, who excelled in *Hanshuli Banker Upakatha*, gave an excellent performance as Arjun Mandal. Unfortunately for him, the Best Actor Award at the National Film Awards was instituted only in 1967. Otherwise, he would have been a strong contender for it. Sanjeev Kumar who played the same role in Hrishikesh Mukherjee's Hindi version, *Arjun Pandit*, however, went on to win the Filmfare Award for the Best Actor in 1977.

In 1967, Tapan started work on a novel by Banaphool, *Hatey Bazarey*. Written as a mélange of experiences of a mofussil doctor, the broader narrative also depicts the everyday life of a somewhat backward region in independent India. The loose structure of the original posed problems during the scriptwriting process. This was also the first time Tapan had to cast stars from Bombay in his film. He took the risk of casting theatre doyen Ajitesh Bandopadhyay in a pivotal villainous role. Ajitesh had played a minor part in

Film booklet cover, *Upahar*, 1955 (*Sounak Gupta*)

Film booklet cover, *Khaniker Atithi*, 1959 (*Sounak Gupta*)

Film booklet cover, *Kabuliwala*, 1957 (*Sounak Gupta*)

Soumitra Chatterjee in *Jhinder Bandi*, 1961 (*Sukumar Roy*)

Soumitra Chatterjee as Mayurbahan in *Jhinder Bandi*, 1961 (*Sukumar Roy*)

Arundhati Devi in *Kshudhita Pashan*, 1960 (*Shoma A.Chatterji*)

Film booklet cover, *Hanshuli Banker Upakatha*, 1962 (*Sounak Gupta*)

Film booklet cover, *Jotugriha*, 1964 (*Sounak Gupta*)

Poster, *Atithi*, 1965
(*Shoma A. Chatterji*)

Poster, *Galpa Holeo Satyi*, 1966
(*Shoma A. Chatterji*)

Film booklet cover, *Hatey Bazarey*, 1967 (*Sounak Gupta*)

Film booklet cover, *Ekhoni*, 1971
(*Sounak Gupta*)

Film booklet cover, *Raja*, 1975
(*Sounak Gupta*)

Film booklet cover, *Sabuj Dwiper Raja*, 1979 (*Sounak Gupta*)

**TOP:** Poster, *Bancharamer Bagan*, 1980 (*Shoma A. Chatterji*); **BOTTOM:** Mahua Roychoudhury and Amol Palekar in *Aadmi Aur Aurat*, 1982 (*Shoma A. Chatterji*)

LEFT: Tanuja in *Adalat O Ekti Meye*, 1982; RIGHT: A still from the film (*Shoma A. Chatterji*)

A still from *Atanka*, 1986 (*Sukumar Roy*)

Poster, *Atanka*, 1986 (*Shoma A. Chatterji*)

Irrfan Khan and Pankaj Kapur in *Ek Doctor Ki Maut*, 1991 (*Shoma A. Chatterji*)

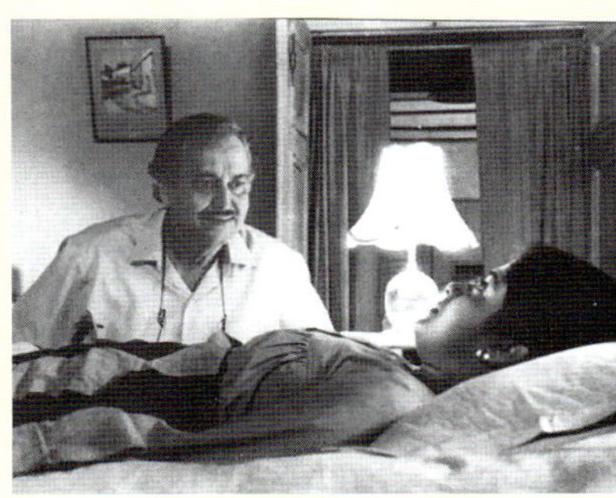

Soumitra Chatterjee in *Wheel Chair*, 1994 (*Sukumar Roy*)

Tapan's *Atithi*, but *Hatey Bazarey* was his first major foray in films, playing one of the most vicious villains in Bengali cinema. Tapan pulled off some notable casting coups on the Bengali screen—Soumitra Chatterjee as the villain in *Jhinder Bandi*, Ajitesh Bandopadhyay as the villain in *Hatey Bazarey*, Rabi Ghosh as the protagonist in *Galpa Holeo Satyi*. Like Ray, Tapan had a gift for spotting acting talent. As a result, most of his films boast of phenomenal acting standards. Tapan also introduced a host of theatre actors including Rudraprasad Sengupta and Chinmoy Roy to the screen. They remain important names in Bengali cinema.

For the central character of the doctor in *Hatey Bazarey*, Tapan had Ashok Kumar in mind right from the time he read the original work: "When Ashim Dutta of Priya Cinema made me an offer to make a film for them, *Hatey Bazarey* was what came to mind. As for the lead role, Ashok Kumar's face surfaced every time. Earlier, Ashim's father, Nepal Dutta, had produced *Chandrasekhar* (1947), a film by Debaki Kumar Bose with Ashok Kumar and Kanan Devi in the lead ... I wrote the script for *Hatey Bazarey* and went to Bombay to meet Ashok Kumar ... He liked it and told me, 'Call me after seven days. I will give you continuous shooting dates. But don't let my secretary know, otherwise he will jeopardise everything by scheduling the shoot of a Hindi film within these dates.' ... After hearing about my interest in casting Vyjayanthimala, Ashok Kumar himself scheduled an appointment with her over the phone and insisted that she work with me. Vyjayanthimala also liked the script. She only asked me, 'Will you dub my voice since I don't know Bangla?' I told her that I wouldn't. After returning to Calcutta, I sent her two cassettes with her dialogues—one recorded at slow speed and the other at medium."[15]

Not only did Tapan extract the required vivacious innocence and rustic naiveté from Vyjayanthimala for her portrayal of Chhipli, a simple village girl, he also made the star from Bombay sing a song for the film! "I did sing a song even though the playback was already done ... While I was rehearsing the lines all by myself quite loudly, I did not notice Tapan-da was standing behind me, listening to me. To my surprise, he told me that I sing very well. Why couldn't I sing the song myself, it would be so natural then! I said, 'God! I am no singer and how could I sing, that too a Bengali song, when I had never sung anything even in my Hindi films?' But Tapan-da did not give up easily. He said he would record the song in my voice and assured me that if I was not happy or satisfied, he would not use it ... Anyway, I mustered the courage and sang the song tuned by Tapan-da. The best part was that my song remained in the film," recalls Vyjayanthimala. [16] The song sounded completely effortless. In the same year, it found a place in an HMV yearly album of songs compiled from all over India.[17]

*Hatey Bazarey* had a deep Bhagalpur connection—Tapan, Banaphool and Ashok Kumar had all spent a substantial part of their lives in the city. Working with Ashok Kumar was an unforgettable experience for Tapan due to the legend's unparalleled devotion to natural acting. "There was a scene with a microscope in *Hatey Bazarey*. So that he didn't look like a novice, he took pains to practise with it for hours. The role required the doctor to apply bandages. To look like a veteran and an experienced doctor, he discussed this with a qualified compounder and picked up the right technique. Only then did he consider himself ready for a shot," Tapan recalled [18].

A major part of the shooting was done in Bhutan. Ashok Kumar was seriously unwell at that time. He had a bout of asthma attacks and the renowned Dr. Mani Chhetri was sent to the location by the then Chief Minister of West Bengal, Prafulla Sen, to attend to him. This was a critical snag in the tight shooting schedule considering the shoestring budget within which Tapan operated as always. Ashok Kumar was advised rest for a few days. Tapan adjusted his plan for the shoot after reconciling to the fact. "On the morning of the second day, I was readying the team for shooting without him. However, I found Ashok Kumar ready to start as well. He told me, 'Let me be clear, either you let me work or you send me back to Bombay.' So we went ahead and started shooting. To my surprise, I saw that he was distinctly uneasy because of his breathing problem, but that was only till the time he had to give a shot. The moment he was in front of the camera, all the physical discomfort vanished from his face and body, and back came his effervescent smile. Using his expressive eyes to great effect, he gave a deeply meaningful performance."[19]

Ashok Kumar successfully portrayed a benevolent country doctor without making the characterisation sentimental or melodramatic. In this film too, the individual's fight against a corrupt system (local businessmen, rich, powerful and lecherous men) and his triumph against the odds in order to uplift the downtrodden is paramount. Tapan's belief in the loner's strength of character and the heights one can achieve if one's goals are selfless and unwavering is emphasised. The mass appeal of both the stars from Bombay and the deeply sensitive story made *Hatey Bazarey* a big commercial hit. It also bagged the

President's Gold Medal for the Best Feature Film in 1967 at the National Film Awards.

In 1968, with *Aponjon,* Tapan presented a masterpiece on the crisis of human values and ethics. Like in *Jotugriha*, the urban middle class is in focus here again. But, rather than generalising the contemporary through the prism of a particular couple, Tapan's spectrum is more generic and all-encompassing. With *Sagina Mahato* (1970) and *Ekhoni* (1971), Tapan's cinema seemed polemical if not political for the first time, as he started to look closely at the angst of the changing times and the ethos of contemporary existential uncertainties.

## REFERENCES

[1] Nandan Mitra, *Tapan Sinha-r Film-making*, Chalachitra o Sanskriti Charcha Kendra, January 2015, p. 60 [Translation by the author]

[2] Tapan Sinha, *Aamar Jiban Aamar Chhabi Vol. I*, Compiled by: Asishtoru Mukhopadhyay, Abhijato Publishing, May 1998, p. 62 [Translation by the author]

[3] Ibid., p. 71

[4] Tapan Sinha, 'A Controlled and Talented Actor', *Soumitra*, Edited by Alok Chattopadhyay and Manas Chakraborty, Sristi Prakasani, 2000, pp. 51–52 [Translation by the author]

[5] Amitava Nag, *Beyond Apu, 20 Favourite Film Roles of Soumitra Chatterjee*, HarperCollins India, 2016, pp. 18–19

[6] Nandan Mitra, *Tapan Sinha-r Film-making*, Chalachitra o Sanskriti Charcha Kendra, January 2015, pp. 66–67 [Translation by the author]

[7] Tapan Sinha, *Aamar Jiban Aamar Chhabi Vol. I*, Compiled by: Asishtoru Mukhopadhyay, Abhijato Publishing, May 1998, p. 91 [Translation by the author]

[8] Ibid., p. 95

[9] Nandan Mitra, *Tapan Sinha-r Film-making*, Chalachitra o Sanskriti Charcha Kendra, January 2015, p. 34 [Translation by the author]

[10] Tapan Sinha, *Chalachchitra Ajibon*, Ed: Shamik Bandopadhyay, Dey's Publishing, 2009, p. 216 [Translation by the author]

[11] Ibid., p. 102

[12] 1965 Interfilm award, Locarno Film Festival Archives website, http://archive.pardo.ch/details.do?methodcall=premiDetails&oc=525331 accessed on 15 March 2018

[13] Tapan Sinha, *Chalachchitra Ajibon*, Ed: Shamik Bandopadhyay, Dey's Publishing, 2009, p. 478 [Translation by the author]

[14] Tapan Sinha, *Aamar Jiban Aamar Chhabi Vol. I*, Compiled by: Asishtoru Mukhopadhyay, Abhijato Publishing, May 1998, p. 106 [Translation by the author]

[15] Tapan Sinha, *Chalachchitra Ajibon*, Ed: Shamik Bandopadhyay, Dey's Publishing, 2009, pp. 318–319 [Translation by the author]

[16] Nandan Mitra, *Tapan Sinha-r Film-making*, Chalachitra o Sanskriti Charcha Kendra, January 2015, p. 71

[17] Tapan Sinha, *Chalachchitra Ajibon*, Ed: Shamik Bandopadhyay, Dey's Publishing, 2009, p. 104 [Translation by the author]

[18] Ibid., p. 32

[19] Ibid., p. 105

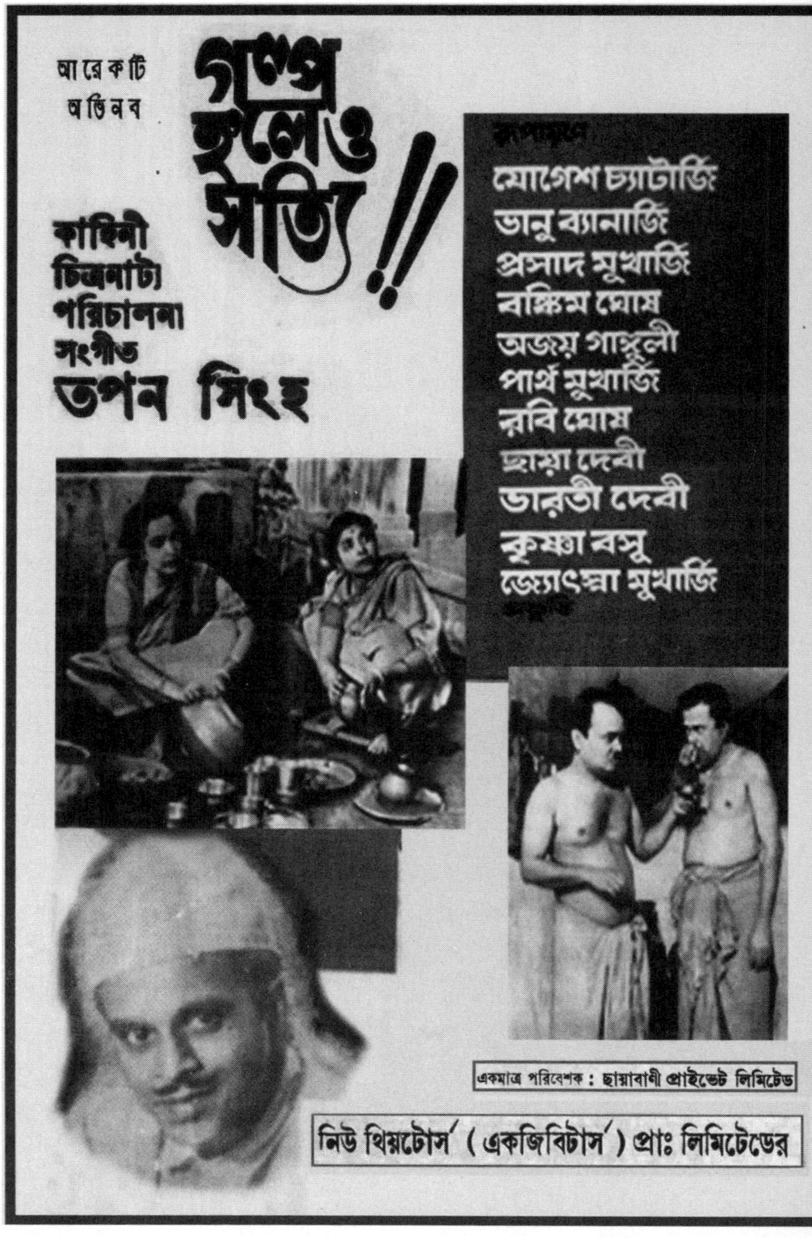
আরেকটি
অভিনব
গল্প হলেও সত্যি!!
কাহিনী
চিত্রনাট্য
পরিচালনা
সংগীত
তপন সিংহ
যোগেশ চ্যাটার্জি
ভানু ব্যানার্জি
প্রসাদ মুখার্জি
বঙ্কিম ঘোষ
অজয় গাঙ্গুলী
পার্থ মুখার্জি
রবি ঘোষ
ছায়া দেবী
ভারতী দেবী
কৃষ্ণা বসু
জ্যোৎস্না মুখার্জি
একমাত্র পরিবেশক : ছায়াবাণী প্রাইভেট লিমিটেড
নিউ থিয়েটার্স (এক্জিবিটার্স) প্রাঃ লিমিটেডের

# Dealing with Contemporary Reality

In 1966, for his fifteenth feature film, *Galpa Holeo Satyi*, Tapan wrote the story himself. Rabi Ghosh, who was considered a mere sidekick comedian till then, got to play the central character of the house help in the film. Ghosh went on to consolidate his position as a character actor later on, mainly with Ray's epic *Goopy Gyne Bagha Byne* (The Adventures of Goopy and Bagha, 1969). *Galpa Holeo Satyi* is one of Tapan's most well-made films. The satire in it is well-conceived and subtle. The film lets us understand the world of Tapan Sinha with stunning clarity.

The seventies were a cauldron of student protests, ideological crises, the Vietnam War (though it started a decade earlier, its international significance peaked in this decade) and the popularity of guerrilla warfare courtesy Che Guevara. It was the time of angst and youth power, the time to overthrow age-old traditions and ideals. In India as well, the pressure was building up with the fourth General Elections slated for 1967. The undisputed supremacy of the Indian National Congress started crumbling as the Congress government was unable to control the food crisis, rising prices of basic commodities and unemployment. The country in general and West Bengal in particular were also secretly getting ready for a peasant uprising in the tea gardens of the northern part of the state, which would soon snowball into the Naxalite revolution.

With respect to Bengali cinema, Ray was still working on his 'classical' films, though a faint reflection of the times can be seen in his *Nayak* (The Hero, 1966) for which he wrote the story himself. Ritwik Ghatak, on the other hand, did not make any films for a while after *Subarnarekha* (The Golden Thread, 1962). The contemporary political situation was reflected much later in his last feature *Jukti, Takko aar Gappo* (Reason, Argument and a Story, 1974). Only Mrinal Sen responded to the needs of the time more directly with his *Pratinidhi* (1964) and *Akash Kusum* (1965). Keeping this background in mind, we can explore the reasons that prompted Tapan to write *Galpa Holeo Satyi* and film it.

In an interview, while speaking about Bengali comedies in general and the making of *Galpa Holeo Satyi* in particular, Tapan elaborated, "I think Bengalis lack a sense of humour. They get angry easily or become upset and unhappy. But the humour quotient is less ... In contrast, the British have a better sense of humour. The greatest entertainers of the 20th century are undoubtedly Charlie Chaplin, Agatha Christie and P. G. Wodehouse ... If we ask for the definition of slapstick, it will be that 'slapstick always rests on absurdity'. Shall we then question, 'Where is the logic in it?' The point is comedy doesn't necessarily care for logic. We are not trained as an audience. The audience is made to view the world through one window. But that doesn't work. Unless you open all the windows, you will never develop a global perspective."[1]

Even within the satirist mode, Tapan did chip in with images of the changing times. For instance, the publicity manager in *Galpa Holeo Satyi* lectures the otherwise 'progressive' young intellectual: "This is an age of S-cube—sex, sadism and shock. Every male commodity has to be advertised using the female body. In every form of art, be it literature, painting, music or cinema, you have to constantly shock people. Remember, the old concepts like Neorealism are passé now. Even Nouvelle Vague is old. What rules and will rule today's world is shockumentary." On the other hand, the third brother of the family, a fretful schoolteacher, announces to his nephew: "We can eat because America is funding food" and to his leftist colleague: "All politicians are opportunists". The CPI(M) drove the formation of the United Front government in Bengal in 1967 after the Indian National Congress lost the mandate in several Indian states in that election.

Tapan's own apolitical positioning, which veered towards left-agnostic had a telling effect on how he was critically received by the Bengali intellectual cultural class and the critics. While he remained very viable at the box office for over three decades, his sway over the critics (the majority of whom remained left-inclined) waned substantially over the years. Ray also voiced his apolitical philosophy consistently, but the awe that he generated among cultural practitioners and scholars is incomparable even today. It is no surprise that Tapan, who was on good terms with those in power till the mid-sixties, soon found himself being given the cold shoulder. Ironic as it may seem, the whole idea of a symbolic Renaissance man appearing from nowhere and disappearing likewise before putting a warring household in order was too simplistic for the communist mindset of the authorities at the time.

The final reference to the family as an ideal utilitarian community in *Galpa Holeo Satyi* is indeed in line with

Marxist philosophy. Yet, given his faith in the concept of self-realisation and the awakening of the individual without the aroma of class-struggle lectures and propaganda meant that Tapan would plow a lonely furrow in the upheavals that marked the era.

In 1968, after *Hatey Bazarey,* Tapan made *Aponjon* on the ongoing lumpenisation of the youth. The first strains of the Naxalbari uprising had already started to unsettle the life of citizens by then. The instability in governance added to the uncertainties as lawlessness broke loose. *Aponjon* takes a slice-of-life look at the city of Calcutta with two youth groups engaged in bitter rivalry over gaining supremacy on the locality they want to rule. Soon they are backed by rival political parties and their path to corruption is secured. Along with the two leaders, Rabi and Chheno (played by newcomers Swarup Dutta and Samit Bhanja respectively), there is also Anandamayee, an aged widow who leaves her rural home and lands up in the city.

The original story had Anandamayee's plight as the central theme. Tapan introduced the characters of Rabi and Chheno based on a personal experience: "One morning two or three ruffians of my locality came to meet me. They wanted me to get Hemanta Mukhopadhyay to sing at one of their musical *jalsa* (concerts). I told them, 'He is a professional and I can't request him to sing at such concerts for free.' Then they brought out a lot of money from a bag and told me, 'We will pay him. Whatever he asks we are ready to pay.' I was very surprised to see so much money. I asked them where they had got it from. They laughed and said, 'Elections are round the corner. It's all a game of money.'

"Then they mentioned the name of a political leader who was allegedly funding them handsomely for doing propaganda for him ... I asked, 'Now that you are dealing with so much money, what will happen when the election gets over?' They looked at me blankly and then said, 'We were promised jobs. But then again none of them recognise us after the elections get over. We will see what happens when the time comes' ... I wondered what would become of these jobless youth once their source of income dried up. They would develop a spending habit and suddenly realise that they didn't have the money to sustain it. Maybe they would be forced to engage in anti-social activities. The reason for the birth of anti-social elements is political leaders or others who use jobless young men for their own petty benefits."[2]

Tapan became an eyesore to the political leaders of the state once again: "The audience loved the film. But I fell out of favour with some of the top political leaders. They started spreading the rumour that I was funded by the CIA (Central Intelligence Agency of the United States federal government) to make the film. Anyway, the film bagged the award for the Best Feature Film in Bengali at the National Film Awards." [3]

In a pivotal scene in *Aponjon*, the political leader Haru Chakraborty is seen tutoring Chheno, the anti-social: "If you read history, you will understand: who removed the kings? Their own zamindars. Who removed the zamindars then? The capitalists. Who is trying to dethrone the capitalists now? It is us. We have become leaders of the masses by preaching about democracy and socialism. Whatever pomp and prosperity kings used to enjoy, we also enjoy the same. There is no difference."

Obviously, dialogues such as this did not go down well with the authorities. But 50 years later, Tapan's analysis and observations seem even more meaningful and powerful due to their directness. Film critic Abesh Kumar Das is unrelenting in his support of Tapan's 'political' idiom. He comments, "With Haru Chakraborty's dialogue Tapan Sinha puts feudalists, capitalists and communists in the same bracket."[4]

*Aponjon* has a number of flashbacks of Anandamayee's youth when we see her husband collecting money for a social cause or the couple providing shelter to a freedom fighter. This is no coincidence. It is Tapan's deliberate ploy to reveal how the hard-earned fruits of the freedom struggle and other social movements went to waste in the late sixties due to the corrupt political figures who purposefully bred the alarming lumpen culture in West Bengal and other parts of India.

Three films, *Pratidwandi* (The Adversary, 1970), *Seemabaddha* (Company Limited, 1971) and *Jana Aranya* (The Middleman, 1975), constitute Ray's famous *Calcutta Trilogy*. Mrinal Sen also directed his trilogy—*Interview* (1971), *Calcutta 71* (1971) and *Padatik* (The Guerrilla Fighter, 1973)—during the same timespan, vividly reflecting the changing ethos of a confused metropolis. Tapan too has a trilogy of sorts on the city with *Aponjon* (1968), *Ekhoni* (1971) and *Raja* (1975).

In *Aponjon,* though Chheno is shown as an uneducated man and a thug, Rabi is educated. Rabi suffers from middle-class confusions while Chheno is apparently free of them. In contrast, the group of young students in *Ekhoni* is a self-reliant if not affluent entity right from the start. *Ekhoni* opens with a cricket match, with the players kitted out in proper clothes and gear. Cricket was still a game of the upper-class and not as commonplace as it is today. Tapan's aim was to portray the growing self-centred aloofness of the youth of the time, especially the upper middle class. He had already dealt with their lumpenisation in *Aponjon*.

This is why we find the student group in *Ekhoni* meeting endlessly at the Calcutta Coffee House, lost in aimless squabbling and *adda* (chat), a Bengali staple. Yet, Arun realises: "We are endlessly talking all the time. But funnily, we don't wish to understand each other's words. Then what is the use of talking so much? Just a stream of sounds, a group of meaningless words, isn't it?" Just like the politician's speech in *Aponjon*, this observation seems more pertinent in today's world of social media and mobile phones where we constantly share our thoughts without pondering over them.

Abesh Kumar Das rightly draws a parallel between Ray's *Pratidwandi* and Sinha's *Ekhoni*: "The aimless solitude is also the main theme of Ray's *Pratidwandi*. In the film, the communist brother Tunu tells his elder brother Siddhartha, the protagonist, 'You don't even have a path to follow … ' His friend who steals all the donations from a box marked 'Red Cross' justifies his actions shamelessly, 'The whole country is going down, brother. If I don't descend as well, shall I remain suspended in air?' In the context of time, the individuality of the characters and their growing loneliness are of immense importance since they are situated at the start of the seventies. Leftist ideals and vision were spreading rapidly in the minds of the Bengali youth then. Against the tide of time Tapan's *Ekhoni* or Ray's *Pratidwandi* actually tell the story of the growing aloofness of modern man."[5] In spite of the characters' individuality, in the last scene of *Ekhoni*, a top shot, Arun and his girlfriend Urmi merge into a crowd of pedestrians. With a deft touch, Tapan suggests Arun could be any educated youth of the city at the time whose material future was bleak even if his love life was firmly anchored.

The streets of the city recur in all the films in Tapan's trilogy. Shots of processions, strikes and posters on the walls depict the political unrest of the time. While *Ekhoni* ends with a street shot, *Raja* opens with a procession on the street. *Raja* is the harshest of the trilogy. The warring teams in *Aponjon* are thugs as well but Rabi is relatively a late convert (post college). Chheno is more raw and uninhibited than him. Raja, on the other hand, is a school dropout who has experienced the crude realities of life up close. The film generated controversy due to its depiction of contemporary society and the allegedly 'foul' language mouthed by the protagonists.

Tapan was prepared to accept the criticism: "I knew there would be criticism. The original story was Prafulla Roy's but I added one thing to it. I had read interview-based reporting in *Anandabazar* on the rise of prostitution in our society. I added that to the script. There was tremendous unrest in society due to financial constraints, old ideals were breaking down, and young girls were falling prey to perverted desires. I knew many would not be able to tolerate such naked depiction. But one can't sit idle and do nothing. As a film-maker I have a social responsibility as well."[6]

In Ray's *Jana Aranya*, a film made at the same time, the protagonist Somnath who was better educated than Raja met a similar fate too. Both characters had to ferry young girls from the outskirts of Calcutta to rich businessmen who were staying in posh hotels in the heart of the city. After *Aponjon* and *Ekhoni*, the question naturally popped up: why did Tapan make *Raja* at all? He definitely wanted to say something more than what he had articulated in the first two. In a short article written at the time of making *Raja*, Tapan explained why he took up the subject and what prompted him to include it in his own *Calcutta Trilogy*: "In our country, specifically in the cities and their outskirts, I can't recall seeing any film dealing with the lower middle class and the lower class. At least I haven't done any significant work on these strata. The condition of today's lower middle class worries me a lot. Different forms of pressure from all quarters have made their existence precarious. The class itself is on the verge of disintegration."[7]

In between *Aponjon* and *Ekhoni,* Tapan made *Sagina Mahato*, one of his most ambitious films. If *Jukti, Takko aar Gappo* portrays Ghatak's political identity in its barest form, *Sagina Mahato* does the same for Tapan. Undoubtedly, his questions about the role of the communist regime and the trade unions sent all the wrong signals to those in power. If the *Calcutta Trilogy* was reflective, *Sagina Mahato* was direct and brutal. The news about Tapan filming *Sagina Mahato* spread quickly and midway into it, he started getting political threats: "I didn't pay heed to the threats that I used to receive at that time. After the film got the censor certificate, rumour had it that it would not get released and cinema halls releasing it would be picketed. Keeping the producer's interests in mind, we arranged for a special show and invited several people from different political parties to it. The representatives of the extremist groups whom we feared the most came up to me and said, 'This is a fantastic film. You have unmasked the hypocrisy of the trade union movement. Go ahead and release the film. We will see what happens next, we are with you.' There were no further problems. On the day of the release, I sensed eight to ten young men shadowing me from a distance. During the interval, when the audience wanted to greet and congratulate me, the men cordoned me off in a sense and whispered: 'Don't let them come close. Who knows what they have in mind?' While the so-called communists were suspicious of the film, it went on to receive the Afro-Asian Award at the Moscow Film Festival."[8]

Siddhartha Kumar Ghosh recalls: "Tapan had great regard for the then Chief Minister of West Bengal, Mr. Jyoti Basu who liked to see his films. I know of special screenings that were arranged for the CM. When the release of *Sagina Mahato* was stalled, Mr. Basu stepped in. Tapan told me that the CM ensured the release went smoothly. Mr. Basu had already watched the film. The entire thing was handled very quietly. Tapan respected Mr. Basu's pragmatism. This is what he identified as able governance."

Tapan roped in Dilip Kumar and Saira Bano to play the central characters in *Sagina Mahato*. Sagina was a challenging role for Dilip Kumar and he essayed it flawlessly. Sagina is an uneducated labour leader at a tea estate in north Bengal who eventually becomes a pawn in the hands of the trade union leader Aniruddha. Aniruddha comes across as a vile person with evil intentions. In the name of providing political support, he sabotages the entire labour uprising and manages to portray Sagina as the main culprit. Lacking the guile that would help him go free, Sagina succumbs to the treacherous ploy and turns into an enemy of the class of people he had chosen to represent. However, Tapan was not imbalanced in his portrayal of the merits and demerits of the trade union movement. In the film, Anupam Dutta, another union leader, comes across as the epitome of reason and empathy. In a crucial altercation scene between

Anupam and Aniruddha, the former warns: "The party is not a heartless machine. If you don't count the individuals, the party doesn't even exist."

Like Sandip in *Ghare Baire* (*The Home and the World*), the Tagore novel adapted into a film by Ray in 1984, Aniruddha is all talk, mostly vacuous. Like Sandip, he instigates gullible people for his personal gains and uses them to settle private scores with others. If Sandip can be termed a villain among freedom fighters, Aniruddha is the same among trade union leaders whereas Sagina is almost childlike. In multiple establishing shots in the film, Sagina is shown traversing the majestic Himalayan range onboard the famous toy train of Darjeeling. In a way, he reminds us of *Atithi*'s Tarapada, a true child of Nature.

Working with Dilip Kumar was a memorable experience for Tapan. He had heard rumours about the thespian's idiosyncrasies and tantrums. However, as the shooting progressed at Kurseong, the star mingled well with the crew: "As an actor I observed a few things in him which are very rare. For example when a shot was being readied, he would act according to my direction and suggestion. At times, he would very politely request, 'If you kindly permit, I may act the same shot in two more ways. You may choose which one to keep at the time of editing.' I always agreed gleefully. To my utter surprise, he would deliver the same shot three to four times, each completely different from the next, yet the dialogues were the same."[9]

Over and above his acting acumen, the star's benevolent side endeared him to Tapan: "One day, a few people from the local slum came to us and said that the school building was in a shambles. They asked if we could help them out. It was indeed in very bad shape. I asked them how much the repairs would cost. They quoted five thousand rupees. Once we returned to the camp after the day's shoot, Dilip Kumar handed over two thousand to me. He said, 'This is from Saira and me. I can pay for the entire repairs. But I will be happy if all of us contribute to the cause. I am pretty sure that you will cherish this one day as well.' We handed over the money to the concerned people. After about three months, when I returned to the same shooting location, I saw a renovated school building there."[10]

In 1977, Tapan made *Ek Je Chhilo Desh* (Once There was a Country), which is a satirical science-fiction film, Tapan's only attempt at this genre. Frustrated with the rampant corruption and erosion of values in social and public life, most directors of the time addressed this crisis in their films. Keeping this as the central theme, Tapan experimented with form and style in *Ek Je Chhilo Desh*.

In 1980, he adapted Manoj Mitra's play *Sajano Bagan* (The Decorated Garden) into the film, *Banchharamer Bagan*. Tapan had never adapted a play before. Interestingly, *Sajano Bagan* was being regularly staged during the making of *Banchharamer Bagan*. Tapan and Arundhati Devi had both watched the play and liked it. Tapan was attracted to it primarily because it dwelt on his favourite theme—an individual's protest against oppression, in this case, in the form of the zamindari system. Playwright Manoj Mitra, who essayed the main character of Banchharam on stage, did the same in the film as well, becoming another successful import from stage to screen in Tapan's cinema.

Mitra says, "We all know that the haves always exploit the have-nots. But the fun element in this play is that the wheel of fortune is reversed here. What if the poor farmer gets a monthly payment from the zamindar? Everyone wants to hear the story of resurrection of a man without any hope. ... In Banchharam's resurrection, people realised that if we could snatch away money from our exploiters, it may be a form of revenge. This creates a wish fulfilment for everyone ... The film was screened at the 1980 Delhi Film Festival. Dipankar Dey and I were put up in the same hotel. One morning, an old man came to visit us. He gave us flowers and told us that he was a cancer patient. After watching the film, he had felt inspired and he wanted to live again. He hoped that he would be able to rise above his hapless situation like Banchharam."[11] *Banchharamer Bagan* was a huge hit in West Bengal as people could relate to the wish fulfilment portrayed in the story.

Tapan encountered a personal glitch while making the film—an unnecessary misunderstanding with Uttam Kumar: "Uttam had been keen on doing a good film for quite some time. He shared his wish with me as well. When I was planning to make *Banchharamer Bagan*, I thought of Uttam as the tyrant zamindar, a role later played by Dipankar Dey. I first offered the role to Uttam and he was a bit sceptical since he hadn't played a part like this before. He took some time and then gave me his available dates. I planned the shoot accordingly and gave dates to the other artists. Uttam suddenly wanted to change the dates, may be because of some Hindi film in Bombay. I told him that the dates couldn't be altered since I had planned the schedule and shared it with all the other artists. Uttam requested me to do the shoot the next month.

"I told him, 'Maybe the others are lesser stars than you, but they also have their own dignity and pride. They may have work next month as well. So it is not possible to postpone the shooting by a month. I think it will be better if you leave the project.' There was a contract with Uttam and an advance had been paid too. After this, there was no response from Uttam. I got busy with the shoot with Dipankar Dey. After I completed it and returned to Calcutta, I came to know that Supriya Devi (Uttam's partner at that time) had moved the court with a complaint against the producer and me ... In the agreement I had with Uttam, it was clearly written that I, as the director, may dismiss the actor any time without citing a reason. No wonder the case was dismissed in court in no time."[12]

Tapan felt very bad about the whole thing since Kumar had been a dear friend right from his *Upahar* days. It was rumoured that the star was very upset too. Tapan wanted to meet Kumar and patch up their differences, but life did not allow it. On 24 July 1980, a black day of Bengali cinema, Uttam Kumar, its biggest superstar ever, passed away. Three months later, *Banchharamer Bagan* was released in Uttara, Purabi and Ujjwala halls.

## REFERENCES

[1] Nandan Mitra, *Tapan Sinha-r Film-making*, Chalachitra O Sanskriti Charcha Kendra, January 2015, p. 19 [Translation by the author]

[2] Tapan Sinha, *Chalachchitra Ajibon*, Ed: Shamik Bandopadhyay, Dey's Publishing, 2009, pp. 319–320 [Translation by the author]

[3] Ibid., p. 320

[4] Abesh Kumar Das, *Tapan Sinha: Sarbik Chalachchitra Biksha*, Sristisukh Prokashan LLP, 2016, p. 25 [Translation by the author]

[5] Ibid., p. 79

[6] Tapan Sinha, *Chalachchitra Ajibon*, Ed: Shamik Bandopadhyay, Dey's Publishing, 2009, p. 322 [Translation by the author]

[7] Ibid., p. 259

[8] Ibid., pp. 321–322

[9] Ibid., p. 45

[10] Ibid., p. 141

[11] Nandan Mitra, *Tapan Sinha-r Film-making*, Chalachitra o Sanskriti Charcha Kendra, January 2015, pp. 92–93 [Translation by the author]

[12] Tapan Sinha, *Chalachchitra Ajibon*, Ed: Shamik Bandopadhyay, Dey's Publishing, 2009, p. 217 [Translation by the author]

চারুচিত্র নিবেদিত
তপন সিংহর ছবি
আতঙ্ক
সৌমিত্র
অনিল
সুমন্ত
শতাব্দী
প্রসেনজিৎ
নির্মলকুমার
মনোজ মিত্র
ভীষ্ম গুহঠাকুরতা
ছায়াবাণী প্রাঃ লিমিটেড
ইস্টম্যানকালার

# The Conscience Trilogy: the Hopeless Paranoia of the Eighties

In an article on the politics of his cinema and his reasons for filming *Raja*, Tapan commented, "Many people tell me that there is a certain amount of 'sweetness' in my cinema even if it deals with harsh realities like in *Aponjon* or *Ekhoni*. I don't deny this. I strongly believe the hopelessness and sorrow that engulf us today are just a passing phase of life. I don't believe that it will remain forever. In other words, I am a die-hard optimist. As a result my characters talk about the rejuvenation of life even within the confines of their present sadness and failures. They don't crumble and lose, they don't forget the value of life and they never give up hope. This is why most of my films have a certain amount of 'sweetness' ingrained in them."[1]

Throughout his career Tapan stayed faithful to this philosophy. In the majority of his films the individual transcends her/himself and characters travel from states of despair or hopelessness to happy times. They also take the audience along with them on this journey. There are elements of wish-fulfilment in most of Tapan's films—the main ingredient of the 'sweetness' he referred to.

From the eighties on, Tapan shifted his techniques and tailored them to a form which was more direct. The 'sweetness' factor was definitely eroded, the central characters would still salvage some hope, but it was limited to themselves. The general audience could relate to the agony of the central characters. Yet, when the films ended, they would be hardly relieved of tension. It was as if the characters in the film had somehow scraped through, leaving the audience with several questions to ruminate on. However, throughout his career, even during the sombre phase, Tapan kept making lighter films. No two successive films were completely similar. Three films deserve special mention in Tapan's serious phase: *Adalat O Ekti Meye* (The Court and a Girl, 1982), *Atanka* (Fear, 1986) and *Antardhan* (The Disappearance, 1992). A salient feature of all three is that they were heavily influenced by newspaper reports and the horrible state of metropolitan life in the City of Joy.

The stories of the first two were written by Tapan himself. The third was based on a short novel by Dibyendu Palit who used news stories as a source for his writing. The fervent mode of these films came as a shock to many, who felt that Tapan was being overtly cynical about contemporary social life. While his *Calcutta Trilogy* addressed the needs of the time, these three seemed ahead of their time. But we can safely club them together and call them the *Conscience Trilogy* since the films remain even more topical and true three decades after their making.

*Adalat O Ekti Meye* revolves around Urmila, a young school teacher who is raped by four college students at the seashore at Gopalpur. It exposes the middle-class facade from behind which people gleefully consume news stories about rape and throng the court premises with the hope of adding some colour to their mundane lives. With brilliant nonchalance, Tapan shows how Urmila is metaphorically raped a second time—by lawyers and the great Indian justice system as she is made to lay herself bare and face questions whose intent is suspect.

In *Atanka*, a retired school teacher witnesses a political murder on a rainy night—his ex-student stabbing a worker of a rival political party. The murderers terrorise the entire locality and the teacher is afraid to approach the police. He reports the murder only after his son is brutally beaten up. This act of courage costs him dearly as the anti-socials pour acid on his daughter's face and disfigures it. In *Antardhan*, the daughter of a retired professor elopes with her fiancé only to find out that her lover is a pimp who uses his looks to lure young girls into the flesh trade. The daughter is eventually reunited with her father but only after she is severely traumatised.

Tapan was a member of the CBFC at this time and was forced to watch a number of C-grade Malayalam films. These were almost pornographic and had explicit scenes of sex and violence. Disgusted with these films, which were rampant at the time, Tapan decided to make a film on rape himself. He recalled: "On hearing my plan Hrishikesh Mukherjee told me, 'You want to make a film on rape! Impossible.' That made me even more determined and I made *Adalat O Ekti Meye*."[2] It got an 'A' certificate, the only film in Tapan's repertoire to have received one. It became a sensation among the audience in the positive sense. A professor at Jadavpur University called up Tapan and told him that even though he and his familywere apprehensive of the film's content before watching it because of its censor rating, they had changed their minds and decided to let their young daughter watch it as well.

In *Atanka*, Tapan's primary objective was to "Try to project a broad enough spectrum of middle-class life as a whole, in a state of crisis … to give back the shock that has shaken me up again and again."[3] *Atanka* too was well received by the audience. But it faced some problems. "At that time, there were many instances of hooliganism by anti-socials. A few of the political leaders were giving them protection. This really enraged me … I made *Atanka* with a lot of anger in me. Soon after, I became anathema for a few leaders of a specific political party … They were of the opinion that crime against women didn't happen in West Bengal. My point was that the state of lawlessness was so alarming that crime against women was just a matter of time. The hint that I dropped in *Atanka* became a reality after a few years in Bantala."[4]

The angst which fuelled Tapan's *Conscience Trilogy* paved the way for the theme of an individual's ascent to enormous mental strength and wisdom in *Wheel Chair*. This again was based on a real-life character—Dr. Mitra, a neurologist who ran a medical home for differently abled patients. Susmita, a vibrant young stenographer was raped in her office premises late one night. Given the neurological disabilities she developed due to the trauma, she was referred to Dr. Mitra's home for treatment. Separated by 12 years, both *Wheel Chair* and *Adalat O Ekti Meye* deal with sexual assault even if the focus and tone of the two are markedly different. In both films, women try to regain their dignity that was temporarily compromised. While Urmila gets her job back and is welcomed by her young students who represent the future, at the end of *Adalat O*

*Ekti Meye*, her battle for justice still continues. In *Wheel Chair,* Susmita avoids a legal battle. In a touching scene she breaks down before her physiotherapist: "I was a simple girl, just a steno typist. Yet, in my humble job, my speed was 45 words per minute. There were never any mistakes, all neat and clean like a printed page. Tell me, can you give me back that strength, that life, those 45 words per minute?" In the end, the image of the wheelchair-bound Susmita acts as a symbol—of hope and mobility, not that of defeat.

Soumitra Chatterjee returned to Tapan's cinema in *Atanka* and went on to play the central character in many of the auteur's films including *Wheel Chair.* He recalls: "The film's shoot was postponed by a few months, which gave me the chance to practise with a wheelchair ... I love sports and know that different physical activities require different kinds of muscular coordination. Just as the coordination required to play cricket and football are different so it is when one moves around in a wheelchair. The results of my detailed practice sessions are evident on the screen."[5]

*Wheel Chair* was Tapan's last significant Bengali film. He did make a few more features and films for television. The significance of Tapan's career rests on the fact that he embraced classical traits early on and as he matured over time as an individual, he continued to experiment with the subjects, and eventually the form, of his films. His literary phase was exemplary, artistically commendable and popular both at the box office and film festivals and competitions. His polemical films have passed the test of time and are referred to and reflected on even today. Some of them provide us with an authentic portrayal of the city of Calcutta of the seventies; many others stun us with their ruthless similarity to the events unfolding in present-day India, decades after they were made.

## REFERENCES

[1] Tapan Sinha, *Chalachchitra Ajibon*, Ed: Shamik Bandopadhyay, Dey's Publishing, 2009, p. 260 [Translation by the author]
[2] Ibid., p. 326
[3] Ibid., p. 449
[4] Ibid., pp. 327–328
[5] Nandan Mitra, *Tapan Sinha-r Film-making*, Chalachitra o Sanskriti Charcha Kendra, January 2015, p. 84 [Translation by the author]

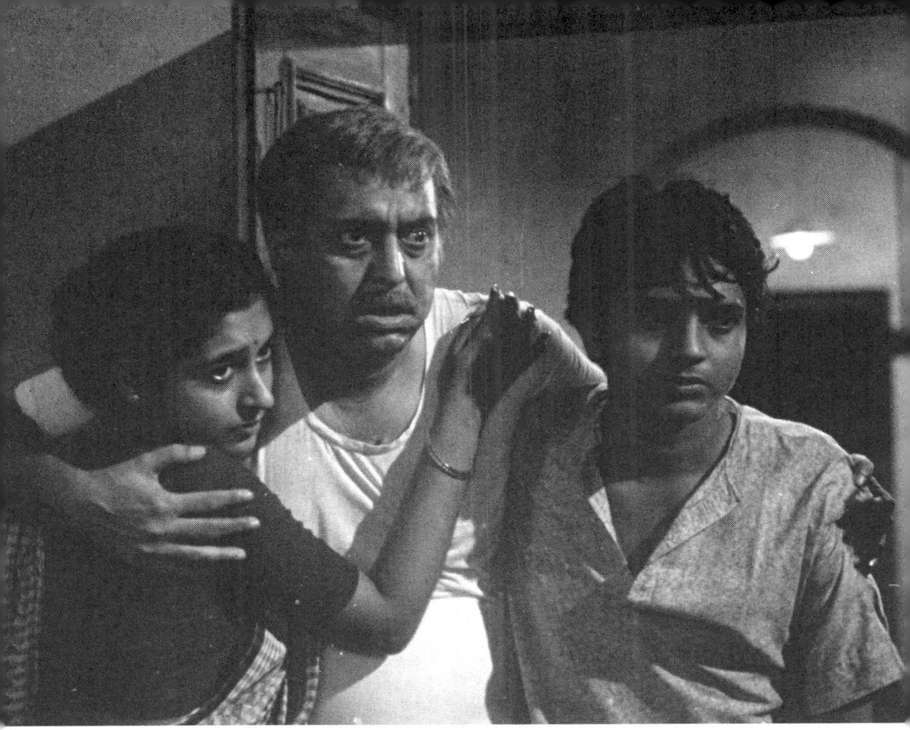

# The Foray into Hindi Films

When Tapan joined the film industry as a technician in the sound department of New Theatres Studio in 1946, he watched Bimal Roy from up close. Roy was a favourite director of Tapan's primarily because of his disciplined working pattern, which Tapan also picked up at Pinewood Studios in England and followed throughout his career with remarkable success. In 1947, when India got freedom and Bengal was partitioned, the market for Bengali cinema was halved overnight. The prosperous Bengali film industry started to decline and the fortunes of New Theatres dwindled. In 1950, Roy moved to Bombay taking along with him a host of technicians who went on to create a niche for themselves in the Hindi film industry.

The Bengali film industry slowly gained momentum in the fifties, with the help of a breed of young film-makers and the popular new on-screen couple, Uttam Kumar and Suchitra Sen. Tapan was part of this group of heritage rebuilders. Hindi cinema was not an option for him. "I have always wished to make my films for the Bengali audience. It is this audience which has taste in literature, idealism and a sense of culture. I wished to provide honest entertainment. Many of my films have been noted and referred to by three generations. What more can I long for? Can a director wish to achieve any more?"[1]

However, this did not stop his films from being remade. As early as in 1961, Hemen Gupta directed *Kabuliwala* in Hindi with Balraj Sahni in the lead and under the aegis of Bimal Roy Productions. Part of the reason for this can be attributed to the Tagore original itself. However, Tagore was not very popular among film-makers, but Tapan's *Kabuliwala* was a super success, both at the box office and with the critics. So, it makes sense that Roy chose to produce this film. Tapan's third and last film based on a Tagore story, *Atithi*, was remade into *Geet Gaata Chal* (Go on Singing) in 1975 by Hiren Nag. Three decades after Tapan's *Kshudhita Pashan*, Gulzar made *Lekin* (But, 1991) based on the same work of Tagore—even though claiming that he was inspired by Tapan's film may be a bit of a stretch. Alo Sarkar who had directed Uttam Kumar in the thespian's disastrous Hindi production, *Chhoti Si Mulaqat* (Brief Encounter, 1967), made a version of Tapan's *Jhinder Bandi* called *Bandi* (The Prisoner) in 1978. The film had a different contextual setting though, here again, Uttam Kumar played the double role of a prince and a common man. Unfortunately, this film was as much of a disaster as Sarkar's earlier directorial venture.

In 1971, Gulzar made his first feature film, *Mere Apne* (My Own People), which was a Hindi remake of Tapan's *Aponjon*. The lead female role was played by Meena Kumari (one of her last roles). Gulzar says, "My first directorial venture, *Mere Apne*, was a Hindi adaptation of Tapan Sinha's Bengali film, *Aponjon*, which appealed to me because it described the restlessness of the youth in the seventies in an environment when young men and women were without jobs and were resorting to needless violence.

It also tackles the vulnerability of helpless old men and women who are mercilessly exploited by family members. I have fond memories of the film because it gave me an opportunity to work with Meena Kumari."[2]

Gulzar returned to Tapan's oeuvre in 1987 with *Ijaazat*, which was adapted from *Jotugriha*. To Gulzar's credit, he transformed the basic crises of the main characters, introduced a new one and still preserved the charm of the original. *Ijaazat* remains one of the most masterfully woven and sensitive Hindi films to date. The other important film-maker who adapted a couple of Tapan's films into Hindi was none other than Hrishikesh Mukherjee. Mukherjee had been Tapan's friend since the New Theatres days and both treaded similar paths of providing entertaining art while experimenting in creative terms. Mukherjee made *Arjun Pandit* based on *Arohi* and *Bawarchi* on *Galpa Holeo Satyi*. *Bawarchi*, which featured superstar Rajesh Khanna in the lead role, was understandably more high-pitched than the subtle, nuanced Bengali version. The film had more subplots and to meet the expectations of a pan-Indian audience via Hindi cinema, Mukherjee had to make more artistic compromises than Tapan. Mukherjee confessed to this. In an interview published in *Star & Style* in 1977, he lamented: "I am tired of making films where I have to compromise every day, always tense about taking risks with other people's money."[3]

Tapan himself remade two of his own films—*Zindagi Zindagi* adapted from (*Khaniker Atithi*) and *Sagina* (adapted from *Sagina Mahato*). He stayed for nearly two years in Bombay in part to shoot the films, a decision he regretted later on: "It was a tremendous mistake on my part. There is no point in remaking your own film. These have been a waste of time for me. Ray told me exactly the same thing. Actually, I cannot turn down requests from friends. I made *Sagina* on Dilip Kumar's request. *Zindagi Zindagi* was also made based on a request. There was no gain in the end. Neither of the two films fared well at the box office. I was not careful enough in my work ... Regarding *Zindagi Zindagi*, I feel the appeal has a typical 'Bengaliness' to it—the whole idea of the village hospital's doctor and his conflicts didn't get across to the larger audience."[4]

Even before making his first Hindi film, Tapan cast the leading stars of Hindi cinema in his Bengali films—Ashok Kumar and Vyjayanthimala in *Hatey Bazarey*, Dilip Kumar and Saira Bano in *Sagina Mahato*. This was much before Mrinal Sen cast Hindi film actors in the Hindi movies he made in the late seventies and eighties. Apart from two minor though important roles, Waheeda Rehman as Gulabi in *Abhijan* (The Expedition, 1962) and Simi as Duli in *Aranyer Din Ratri*, Ray never used Hindi stars in his Bengali films. However, Sharmila Tagore remained a part of the Ray crew since she made her debut in Ray's *Apur Sansar*. By getting stars from Bombay to work in Bengali films, Tapan actually broadened the horizons of Bengali cinema in particular and regional cinema in general. This tradition was carried forward by Rituparno Ghosh who also featured the biggest stars of Hindi cinema in his Bengali films.

The first aesthetically fulfilling Hindi venture for Tapan was *Aadmi Aur Aurat* (Man and Woman, 1982), which he made for Doordarshan, an autonomous public service broadcaster founded by the Government of India and the country's lone television channel at that time. The film, which focuses on the journey of a pregnant woman and a young man who carries her to a hospital for her delivery, was taut and precise. Since this was a tele-film, Tapan could work freely, unfettered by commercial aspects: "I felt a sense of freedom because I was making it for national TV, which had asked me to make a film and given me a free hand. I therefore didn't need to think of box-office prospects. I decided to take advantage of this situation and make a film the way I'd love to, and broke away from the kind of films I had been making. You will notice for example the economy of shots in this film. I had often thought of trying this out, but had never dared to, keeping the audience in mind ... The most rewarding part about making a different kind of film was the warm appreciation of the spectators—from Satyajit Ray to the common man."[5]

The film was critically appreciated. Tapan said, "After watching *Aadmi Aur Aurat*, Satyajit-babu wrote to me to say that according to him, this was not only my best film but also one of India's best ever. He took the initiative and wrote a letter to BBC's Channel 4 about the film and they reciprocated with a screening offer to Doordarshan ... The film bagged the award for the Best Feature Film on National Integration at the 32nd National Film Awards, 1985."[6] Despite the accolades, Tapan was self-critical and perpetually in doubt about his work: "There are several aspects to a film. After watching *Aadmi Aur Aurat*, I felt it would have been much better without a background score. There were already a number of sounds and natural music. For example, the cows on the mountain had small bells around their necks, which chimed sweetly as they moved around. That chiming alone could have been an excellent sound effect. Similarly, the flowing water in the river created a different yet marvellous sound effect. I felt later that the story was not narrated in the proper way or maybe the problem was that of cinematography (no fault of the cinematographer's). The mistake was mine since I insisted on the type of lens or filter to be used, and the edit pattern of the film."[7]

Mahua Roychoudhury gave a scintillating performance in the film as did Amol Palekar. Palekar's role remains a distinct departure in his varied oeuvre. He mentioned a minor incident that showcased Tapan's perfectionist attitude: "When we shot the last scene of the film, I could not summon any tears—I was too tired and dried up emotionally. So there were 3–4 retakes. Tapan-da okayed the last one though I was not satisfied with it. The next morning, we were scheduled to shoot a scene in a different location with a crowd. As I was getting ready for it, Tapan-da suddenly announced a retake of the previous night's shot. I was taken aback. He simply said, 'Amol, don't think, discuss or argue. Just give the shot.' As the camera rolled, I managed to cry even without using glycerin. He clapped for me and hugged me. His eyes were moist when he said, 'How could I let my hero be dissatisfied?'"[8]

Tapan remade *Aadmi Aur Aurat* into *Manush* (Human), a Bengali version, for Films Division the very next year. He cast a different set of actors as the central characters in *Manush*.

There is no argument about *Ek Doctor Ki Maut* being Tapan's finest Hindi feature film. Based on Ramapada Chaudhuri's *Abhimanyu*, Tapan had earlier started work on a Bengali film with the same name, with Soumitra Chatterjee and Madhabi Mukhopadhyay, in the lead. He could not complete it after the producer backed out. Chaudhuri's story was based on a doctor-scientist in the mould of the real-life Dr. Subhash Mukhopadhyay whose pioneering research produced India's first test-tube baby. Dr. Mukhopadhyay committed suicide after politics at the national level prevented him from sharing his findings and research with the international community. The news shocked the educated middle class and newspapers delved deep into it as well at that time.

The agony of not finishing *Abhimanyu* (Tapan's only incomplete film) was eventually compensated for by *Ek Doctor Ki Maut*. The fate of the committed and successful individual who was marginalised because he refused to tow the line appealed to Tapan. "Even after conducting successful research on the test-tube baby, the doctor didn't get his due recognition and he committed suicide. I didn't want to show this tragic event. Instead, I showed that the doctor migrated because I feel that in science no one actually dies. Every scientist's work remains. What I wanted to say was that the doctor had to migrate since there is so much politics in academics in India. This migration is nothing but brain-drain and India is deprived of the services of great talent. Over the last few decades, so many brilliant students have left West Bengal and moved to other Indian states. Brain-drain to foreign countries is not the only reality, the same happens between different Indian states as well."[9]

At the 38th National Film Awards, *Ek Doctor Ki Maut* received the awards for the Second Best Feature Film and Best Director. The citation said, "The Award for the Second Best Feature Film of 1990 is given to *Ek Doctor Ki Maut* for making a very relevant social comment, presented in a tremendously communicative yet emotional manner." In the same year, Pankaj Kapur received the Special Jury Award for "having effectively projected the in-built trauma of an aspiring, thinking, creative mind, in the context of a demoralising, fossilised establishment that does not provide scope for fruition of a path-breaking spirit."[10] Shabana Azmi played the role of the wife of the doctor-scientist. This was her first appearance in a Tapan Sinha film: "While working with Tapan-da, I realised he had a keen eye for detail. The character I played was that of the wife of an absent-minded doctor-scientist. The husband doesn't pay any attention to earning money and so their financial condition is poor. My performance was slightly different from what a person in that situation would do. Tapan-da realised it instantly and told me in a low and polite tone: 'Shabana, what you are doing portrays a character who belongs to the class to which Shabana Azmi belongs. This doctor's wife doesn't belong to that class.' I realised my mistake and made changes accordingly. Tapan-da later appreciated my acting very much."[11]

## REFERENCES

[1] Tapan Sinha, *Chalachchitra Ajibon*, Ed: Shamik Bandopadhyay, Dey's Publishing, 2009, p. 334 [Translation by the author]

[2] Gulzar, 'I Want to Learn the Mainstream Language of Cinema', Interview with Shoma A. Chatterji, *India Together*, 5 June 2014. http://www.indiatogether.org/gulzar-interview-after-dadasaheb-phalke-award-people accessed on 15 March 2018

[3] Jai Arjun Singh, *The World of Hrishikesh Mukherjee*, Penguin Viking, 2015, p. 264

[4] Tapan Sinha, *Chalachchitra Ajibon*, Ed: Shamik Bandopadhyay, Dey's Publishing, 2009, p. 334 [Translation by the author]

[5] Ibid., pp. 449–450

[6] Ibid., p. 327

[7] Ibid., pp. 401–402

[8] Nandan Mitra, *Tapan Sinha-r Film-making*, Chalachitra o Sanskriti Charcha Kendra, January 2015, pp. 73–74

[9] Ibid., p. 24

[10] 38th National Film Awards, 1991, http://iffi.nic.in/Dff2011/Frm38thNFAAward.aspx accessed on 15 March 2018.

[11] Shabana Azmi, 'He Trusts Me', *Tapan Sinha Special Issue Chitravas*, Vol. 38 (No. 1–4), January–December 2003, p. 107 [Translation from the Bengali by the author]

সবুজ দ্বীপের
আন্দামানে অ্যাডভেঞ্চার
তপন সিংহ'র ছবি
ইস্টম্যানকালার

# Something for the Young: Children's Films

Children's cinema has never been a popular genre among Indian film-makers. This applies to Bengali cinema as well even though it is a bit puzzling since children's literature in Bengali has always been quite popular. There are two reasons for this—a substantial volume of children's literature in Bengali veers towards fantasy and science fiction and the other focus area is adventure. Both entail a lot of expense and require the involvement of highly skilled art directors who can do justice to the subjects. The best art directors in Indian cinema in general and Bengali cinema in particular prefer to work on other subjects, with documented references to fall back on.

Ray was one director who took up the cause of children's cinema in Bengali with great seriousness. He started writing stories for adolescents since the mid-sixties starring the iconic detective Feluda. He also adapted two of his Feluda stories into films. *Sonar Kella* and *Joi Baba Felunath* became two of the most popular films of Bengali cinema. Tapan's first children's film was *Safed Haathi* (1977) and he was motivated by an idealistic reason to make children's films: "In our country crores of babies are born every year, but there is no cinema for them. The government has set up an organisation for the sake of it, its condition is pathetic. None of the significant directors want to make children's films primarily because there is no money in it. Even if one or two do try, their inexperience in the genre turns the films into disasters. In all civilised countries of the world children's films are made with a lot of care and responsibility, money is not a factor. The objective is to entertain children … In our country, these things have no meaning. I meet a lot of people who complain that we don't make enough films for children. I tell them that we do make films, but you don't take your children to watch them because you adults don't want to sit through them. You forget that children will get honest entertainment that is beneficial for their future from these films."[1]

Entertainment was paramount in Tapan's mind while he was making a film. Children's films were no exception. Recognising the dearth of quality children's films, Tapan decided right from *Safed Haathi* that his mandate would be to entertain his young audience rather than to play a prophet and end up boring them by trying to educate them. He was very clear about his purpose and philosophy. "We have all been their age once. So whatever used to appeal to us when we were young was what I wanted to portray in my children's films. For example, there were many children's magazines when we were young and we used to read the adventure stories in them, which were very good. I used to take off into the world of my imagination thanks to those stories. I think today's children will love it if we drag them out of their apartments in Calcutta and take them to far-off places through my films. This was the idea behind shooting

*Sabuj Dwiper Raja* (King of the Green Island, 1979) entirely in the Andamans. Initially it was meant to be an indoor film. But later on, I thought that children would miss the beauty and excitement of the Andamans if I made an indoor film. I have always thought about entertaining children, I never wanted to educate them through my films"[2]

This is not entirely true though. In *Sabuj Dwiper Raja*, the original story ended with the long-lost freedom fighter returning to Calcutta to witness the state of affairs in post-Independence India. Tapan changed this by keeping him on the islands and intensified the nationalist feeling by introducing "Vande Mataram" (Hail the Motherland) as the background song. *Aaj Ka Robinhood* (Today's Robinhood) too had a message mixed in with the entertainment element. The story revolves around a zamindar in a village and his poor subjects. The children of the zamindar's house study at a private school located in their own home where a poor boy from the slums is made to wait on them. It turns out that the boy has an amazing memory and can retain everything the tutor says in class. Tapan was promoting the philosophy that even if human beings deprive others of their rights, Nature never discriminates.

Tapan's Hindi film, *Safed Haathi,* was loosely based on Herman Melville's *Moby Dick*. It starred nine students from the Film and Television Institute of India (FTII), Pune. The film was shot at locations in different parts of the country on a princely budget of twenty-eight lakh rupees—certainly one of the most extravagant budgets Tapan ever had. The film was declared the Best Children's Film at the 25th National Film Awards. The Award citation read: "For a film which with a quiet realism evokes the fascination and mystery of the jungle; for its mature emphasis on the harmonious relationship between Man and Nature; for the personal empathy portrayed between a child and creatures of the forest; for a story of lyrical charm and gripping adventure, which educates even as it entertains children and grown-ups alike."[3]

However, *Safed Haathi* posed a problem. Distributors were disinterested in a children's film. Dr. Pratap Chandra Chandra, the then Education Minister, watched the film and liked it. He issued a circular to all state governments in India to ensure they followed the central government's policy of tax exemption for children's films or national award winners. The film's producer, R.A. Jalan, recollected: "I went to Bombay to meet the distributors, but they all backed out because this was a film from Calcutta though made in Hindi. Finally, we managed to release it in Bombay with tax exemption. It was released in Ahmedabad as well. There, Dilip Kumar accompanied Tapan-da to the release. The report was very positive and that sent a message to the distributors. The film was eventually released all over India. Ironically, it didn't get tax exemption in Calcutta. However, the certificate from the Ministry of Education, Government of India, helped to get the film screened in schools. It won the National Award as well and was telecast on national television."[4]

As in his other films, Tapan was strict about maintaining acting standards and casting the right people in his children's films. For the role of Sibu, the young boy in *Safed Haathi*, he held auditions with many candidates and finally selected Aswini Agarwal, son of one of the film's co-producers, Pratap Agarwal. Aswini was living in Kurseong at the time. Tapan visited him at home and patiently groomed him to play the role by explaining the story, answering the boy's questions and giving him his dialogues. After his Class IV exams, Aswini went to Calcutta and met Tapan: "He asked me to narrate the dialogues which I did correctly. Then the dialogue writer and Tapan-da broke down the sentences into pieces and taught me how to say them. He sent me with his Assistant Director to Rajganjpur (Orissa) where the Dalmiyas used to keep their two pet elephants. For three days, I had to sleep with the mahout as if I were a family member and get acquainted with one of the elephants. I used to pet it and feed it bananas. As I rode on the elephant's back, I became friendly with it. Tapan-da started the shoot with long shots without any close-ups or dialogues … After three or four days he started taking close-up shots."[5]

The film was shot at locations across India—from the Bandipura Forest in Karnataka to Bomdila Hill in Arunachal Pradesh. The extensive shooting schedule at multiple locations with a big crew and many animals took a toll on Tapan. He suffered a massive heart attack after completing the film. In a 1991 interview with the literary magazine, *Desh,* an anguished Tapan reminisced: "Arundhati Devi was the only person in the house then. At that early hour, she got me to the Intensive Care Unit of Woodlands Nursing Home, Calcutta, within 25 minutes. I was released from there after eight weeks. Within two weeks of my return Arundhati Devi suffered a cerebral stroke, which paralysed the right side of her body. It was a terrible phase in our lives … I feel I am a very selfish and cruel person.

"After these two incidents, we both had to take medicines—one tablet for me and five for her. Every morning, during breakfast, she would keep my tablet ready. I never enquired if she was taking her tablets regularly. Now that she is no more (Arundhati Devi passed away on

16 October 1990) my heart goes out to her. I feel her absence every day, every moment. It was a relationship of 30 years. Now I have become completely alone and lonely. My son Anindya wanted to come and stay with me. But I stopped him. He did his doctorate in Molecular Biology from the Tata Institute of Fundamental Research and is a Research Associate with the Indian Institute of Science. I can't let him ruin his bright career for me."[6]

The heart attack he suffered from after *Safed Haathi* had a telling impact on Tapan. He was a natural athlete and had a good physique as well. The heart attack made him temporarily doubt his own strength and wonder whether he would ever make films again. However, he did make another children's film the next year. Equally important, however unrelated it may seem, is the fact that his hard-hitting *Conscience Trilogy* was filmed shortly after in the eighties. Maybe the heart attack sounded an alarm about an uncertain future and he did not waste any time proving his critics wrong by making polemical films that were less lyrical and more topical.

After the success of *Safed Haathi*, while he was recovering from the trauma of his illness and contemplating a bleak future, V. Shantaram, the legendary film-maker, encouraged Tapan to return to film-making: "Shantaram-ji told me to make another children's film for the Children's Film Society. He also told me to make it in Bengali. I replied that I probably would not be able to direct a film again due to my heart attack. He laughed at me and said that he had suffered three attacks and was still working. He insisted that I should return to work and only that would keep me well."[7] This led to *Sabuj Dwiper Raja* the next year, Tapan's second children's film and his only one in Bengali.

R.A. Jalan, the producer of *Safed Haathi*, requested Tapan to make another children's film in Hindi. He agreed and went on to make *Aaj Ka Robinhood*. The film was made in collaboration with the Children's Film Society because Tapan had a good experience working with the organisation on *Sabuj Dwiper Raja*. The release of *Aaj Ka Robinhood* ran into rough weather in West Bengal just like *Safed Haathi*. Tapan attributed this to the Government of West Bengal's discontent about his earlier film, *Atanka*, in which he exposed the listless governance of the state administration. "Mr. Jyoti Basu (the then Chief Minister of West Bengal) and Mr. Ashim Dasgupta (the then Finance Minister of West Bengal) watched *Aaj Ka Robinhood* and the Government of West Bengal made the film tax free for eight weeks. We appealed to the Department of Information and Broadcasting of the Government of West Bengal to send a circular to schools for bulk booking. This was nothing new and was done for several earlier films as well. But Mr. Buddhadeb Bhattacharya (the then Minister for Information and Broadcasting) rejected our plea summarily and termed this a 'medieval strategy'. He didn't watch the film, nor did he want to understand its subject. This came out in the newspapers as well and editorials were written. I am an outcast to them even now."[8]

Jalan recounted how the film fared outside of Bengal and at film festivals: "When it was selected as the first children's film to be included in the Indian panorama, it created a lot of controversy. There was no clause that said that a children's film could not be selected. After this, the film went to the Berlin Film Festival where it got a special mention."[9] Cinematographer Kamal Nayek, who worked on *Aaj Ka Robinhood*, explained how Tapan would direct the child protagonist: "The boy was all of twelve and he was trained from 6 a. m. for a month before the shooting started. This was because there were many shots of him riding a horse in the film. One day Tapan-da was showing him how he needed to sing spontaneously and walk across a dam. At that time, it was drizzling. We all took cover. Only Tapan-da stood in the rain training the boy for a singing scene. It was a brilliant sight and he was at his best as an acting teacher. I fail to express it in words. I was restless and I filmed this incident, which was later used in a documentary on Tapan-da."[10]

Tapan had a ghastly accident during the shoot of *Aaj Ka Robinhood* which stayed etched on Kamal's mind for long: "The shot involved an elephant. Utpal Dutt was riding it and Rabi Ghosh was standing on the ground next to them. Utpal Dutt was speaking to Rabi-da in the shot. There was a tracking shot in parallel to the path across which the elephant would walk and the camera was on the track. With his back to the camera, Tapan-da was directing the elephant to approach without realising that the animal was getting very close to the camera without maintaining the parallelism. Through the camera, I saw the elephant was getting too close and hence the image was not right. Tapan-da got stuck on the ground when the elephant came close to him. It hit Tapan-da with its trunk and he fell in between its legs. Immobile with shock, we watched helplessly from a distance. The elephant raised one foot to crush Tapan-da when the mahout rushed in and tapped the raised leg with his stick. The elephant turned around immediately and started to run. Utpal-da who was riding the elephant was frightened out of his wits. The mahout eventually got the elephant under control."[11]

Tapan had to be hospitalised after this and film-making became even more difficult for him. His last children's film, *Anokha Moti* (The Magic Pearl, 2000), preached the values of a virtuous life. Aimed at children below 10, the film is especially relevant for the children of today who are living in a cyber age. The emotions and the fundamental values the film contains remain relevant, along with Tapan's simple narrative style—the hallmark of his films.

## REFERENCES

[1] Tapan Sinha, *Chalachchitra Ajibon*, Ed: Shamik Bandopadhyay, Dey's Publishing, 2009, p. 170 [Translation by the author]

[2] Nandan Mitra, *Tapan Sinha-r Film-making*, Chalachitra o Sanskriti Charcha Kendra, January 2015, p. 26 [Translation by the author]

[3] Citation for the Award for the Best Children's Film, *25th National Film Award Catalogue*, http://dff.nic.in/Attachments/Documents/92_25thNfacatalogue.pdf accessed on 15 March 2018

[4] Nandan Mitra, *Tapan Sinha-r Film-making*, Chalachitra o Sanskriti Charcha Kendra, January 2015, p. 181 [Translation by the author]

[5] Ibid., p. 131

[6] Tapan Sinha, *Chalachchitra Ajibon*, Ed: Shamik Bandopadhyay, Dey's Publishing, 2009, p. 324 [Translation by the author]

[7] Ibid., p. 325

[8] Ibid., p. 328

[9] Nandan Mitra, *Tapan Sinha-r Film-making*, Chalachitra o Sanskriti Charcha Kendra, January 2015, p. 181–182 [Translation by the author]

[10] Ibid., p. 65

[11] Ibid., pp. 65–66 [Translation by the author]

প্রিয়া ফিল্মসের নিবেদন
হাটে বাজারে

তপন সিংহের
এখনই

# Tapan Sinha and the Triumvirate of Bengali Cinema

Most serious discussions on Bengali cinema start and end with the holy trinity of Satyajit Ray, Ritwik Ghatak and Mrinal Sen. This is regrettable because in the process the intermediate strands of creative energy which satiate the minds and imagination of the educated, middle-class Bengali are ignored. Directors like Ajoy Kar, Asit Sen and Tarun Majumdar made sure that there was no polarisation within the movie-going audience from the fifties to the seventies in Bengali cinema. The literary flourish of the time and the richness of theatrical productions along with inspired cinematic practice formed the three main vertices on which the spirit of Bengali intellectualism rested. There was homogeneity of cultural preferences within this spectrum. The urban-rural divide and the diversity between audiences belonging to different economic strata were not pronounced in the appreciation of fine arts.

In this milieu, Tapan Sinha occupied a very significant role. He was the link between Bengal's famed troika (Satyajit Ray, Ritwik Ghatak, Mrinal Sen) and their less-celebrated compatriots. Looking back, it seems almost a crime that his films were neglected and almost forgotten due to the lack of literature on them. The initial fifteen years of his career, from his first film *Ankush* till his seventeenth *Aponjon*, have always been appreciated by the daily press and the general audience. Occasionally, his films travelled to foreign film festivals with moderate success. The semi-commercial element of his cinema (positioned somewhere between so-called 'art' films and typical star-based 'commercial' ones) appealed to refined tastes and also scored at the box office.

Our overt obsession with genius, placing it at a higher pedestal than talent, has always been problematic when it comes to analysing art and artists. William Shakespeare was a genius. Rabindranath Tagore was one and so was Satyajit Ray. To compare any film-maker of that era with Ray time and again is to hoodwink our own analytical capabilities. Critics fail miserably when they try to measure everyone using the same lens. This monumental blunder singed all compatriots of Ray but damaged Tapan the most.

Tapan's one limitation as an artistic film-maker probably lay in the fact that unlike the triad, he failed to find a theme to which his aesthetic sensibilities could be tied. He took up diverse subjects for his films, no two subsequent films seemed similar. If that was his strength, it was his tragedy too. Bergman had several repetitive themes in his repertoire, Tarkovsky's frames freeze with the luminance of paintings, Antonioni's explorations of the human soul reverberate in the hearts of viewers, Ozu's stylistic simplicity makes him distant and equally commonplace, Kurosawa's plaintive grandeur pulses with passion, Ghatak's nostalgia for a lost land and time is full of pathos while Ray's subtle wit targeted at the Bengali middle-class holds a mirror before us. What Tapan lacked was such a signature theme, one he could repeat either in style or in narrative symmetry.

It is foolish to assume that Tapan could have emerged differently. His deep roots in the Bengali cultural climate, mainly music and literature, entrenched in him a particular practice of story-telling. The one minor inadequacy was his inability to paint an image through his films. All great film-makers, at home or in the world, have a facility to paint pictures onscreen. In his finest films, Ray envisioned a vast canvas of oil paints. So did Ghatak through the lashing sweeps of his wide-angled frames. Sen never believed in the grand narratives of life. For him, the picture was broken already, and he broke it further to create his own collage of fractured realism. Through his films, Tapan neither made nor attempted to break away from that unattainable image, which lures and fascinates audiences for a lifetime.

Yet, Tapan's mastery as a film-maker has always been recognised by the mass audience though critics seldom understood its relevance. In a culture that thrives on comparison with foreign philosophies and vision, one in which despair and self-pity are paramount, an artist who unabashedly celebrated a somewhat romantic vision of life, where guile ultimately gives way to righteousness, is likely to be thought of as shallow and weak. That is why in most writings on Tapan, he has been praised for providing 'wholesome entertainment'. This was Tapan's purpose, a philosophy he developed based on his fondness for classical Hollywood films. He wanted to provide his audience with an ease of repose, not to agitate them or awaken them to the social problems that plagued their quotidian lives anyway. In the first two decades of his film-making till 1970, this was Tapan's clear intention. Looking back, it is easy to see how with diverse stories, disparate locales and settings, Tapan could successfully attain his goal.

The typical Bengali mindset favours the proverbial 'have-not'. Money, to some extent even today, is equated with having less class and being dishonest. Tapan's box-office successes and modest ambition to entertain his audience rarely impressed armchair critics. The critic, suffering from an inferiority complex about Indian art, was enamoured by accolades and awards from foreign film festivals. Tapan slowly but surely drifted away from the radar of film society activists of the fifties to the seventies. His films were still being appreciated in newspaper reviews but the proliferation of pseudo-intellectual, film-society-influenced apprentices in the ranks of the dailies started to show.

There was another reason for Tapan's animosity towards the Bengali intelligentsia which was rife since the mid-sixties. What was a hint in *Galpa Holeo Satyi* became a statement in *Sagina Mahato*. As the city of Calcutta reeled under revolutionary unrest and being a reactionary (at least in terms of ideology) became fashionable, Tapan's stance was unacceptable for the majority of educated Bengalis who were naturally left-inclined in their political beliefs. Even the darling of film-society critics, Satyajit Ray preferred to keep Tunu, the communist brother of the ambivalent Siddhartha in *Pratidwandi* (a film released in the same year as Tapan's *Sagina Mahato*), out of narrative focus. Meanwhile, Sen went all guns blazing with his overt political messages in *Bhuvan Shome* (1969) and in *Interview* (1970).

Ghatak heaped praises on armed revolution and hailed it as the harbinger of hope, albeit in a bit of a misguided way in his last film, *Jukti, Takko aar Gappo* (1974). During this turbulent time, the other directors with whom Tapan Sinha gets inadvertently bracketed with often by later film critics, were continuing with their earlier brand of film-making. Ajoy Kar made *Parineeta* (1969) and *Malyadan* (1971). After shifting to Bombay, Asit Sen made many tear-jerkers: *Khamoshi* (1969), *Maa aur Mamta* (1970) and *Safar* (1970). Whereas Tarun Majumdar could muster *Nimantran* (1971), *Kuheli* (1971) or at most an adolescent love story *Sriman Prithwiraj* (1973), bolstered by the success of an earlier *Balika Badhu* in 1967.

None of these film-makers, along with the ones more attuned to commercial success, seemed to bother much about the changing times in the political environment of West Bengal. As the state burned, having a political ideology in the arts meant being leftist—any deviation came at your peril. Ray's political ambivalence in his films was criticised as well, but his stature was so untouchable that it was left relatively unharmed. Critics then and even later on mostly failed to realise that Tapan was not uncertain in his message. He had a political statement to make, as strong as a Sen or a Ghatak. His message was just not in vogue at the time.

Tapan's films started to be clubbed with the works of film-makers who were arguably less gifted than him due to the callousness of film scholars and critics who were marking his position in the canon of Bengali cinema. To make matters worse, Tapan's worst decade as a creative artist was the seventies itself. Apart from *Sagina Mahato* and *Ekhoni* no other film of his in this decade was in the same league as the films he had made over the past fifteen years. *Harmonium* (1976) had the promise of the classical drift found in many of his earlier films. Yet, apart from the songs, penned by Tapan himself, the film didn't make a big impression. *Raja*, the last of Tapan's own *Calcutta*

*Trilogy*, was impressive in its basic premise that shows the complete lumpenisation of youth. However, it was arguably the weakest in the trilogy perhaps because Tapan tried to portray a life he didn't know that well.

Tapan's own take on changing urban life was depicted best in his *Calcutta Trilogy* even though he was never given enough credit for it. Tapan, like Ray, was unable to come to terms with the shifting dynamics of middle-class Bengali life. Both of them were more Gandhian in their philosophy than Sen and Ghatak. Sen's ascent was punctuated in the seventies, the same decade both Ray and Tapan fell from the standards they had set for themselves. Ray ventured into children's films twice and so did Tapan.

*Safed Haathi* (1978) was an entertainer for children but the next year's *Sabuj Dwiper Raja* was shabby on all fronts. Both Ray and Tapan, burdened by their utter disillusionment with contemporary reality, the unrest and killings, the soaring cost of living and the blatant erosion of moral values, viewed children as the last ray of hope. With their separate and different Calcutta trilogies, both wished to understand their times. Their approach was pained and the criticism was directed more towards the self than the external adversary. In retrospect, the seventies seemed to have been a creative cooling phase for both Ray and Tapan. Due to his ill health Ray could manage only *Ghare B*aire in the entire eighties apart from the fantasy-cum-satire *Hirak Rajar Deshe* (1980).

Awakening from a creative slumber, Tapan came back much stronger with what I call his *Conscience Trilogy*—*Adalat O Ekti Meye*, *Atanka* and *Antardhan* . Shortly before the trilogy, he had made the hugely successful *Banchharamer Bagan* in 1980, a satire about an old man who refuses to die.

The spirit of Banchharam, the old farmer, is the spirit of Tapan himself and also the ethos of an old-world psyche which refuses to give up hope and retains a romantic vision of the world. As with Tapan, Banchharam's vision is not based on falsehood, rather, he chooses to embrace the positives and gaze at the sun to live a luminous life. Tapan's second phase, which started off in the 1980s, is crucial in understanding his mental makeup as a film-maker.

Just as some trees which grow very well in the initial years turn hideously peculiar with time, so do human beings as they age. Ultimately, we deserve the face and the fate we have as we embellish or denude out histories and that of our families. Many artists, blessed with promise and fortitude pale with time. This does not diminish the glory they earned for their earlier works. But an artist who adapts well is a thinking being, acutely aware of his role in the context of society and time.

A young Tapan turned to classics for the content of his films. These stories have an element of latent harmony. With age, cynicism usually grips the best of us, but Tapan's *Conscience Trilogy* was full of raging angst against society and the system. The anti-establishment traits, however, almost always, culminated in closed endings in his films either on a happy note or occasionally tragic ones. The multifarious ambiguity that marks the works of several extraordinary artists was never Tapan's forte. But within the realms of conventional, narrative storytelling Tapan could expand his boundaries and that of quasi-commercial films. His sensitivities evolved over time as he confined himself to the world of the middle-class which he knew well. His discipline as a film-maker is worth emulating for every newbie. In his subdued attempts at experimentation, his drive to explore different facets of human life, his simple rendition of complex stories, his strong belief in the ultimate nobility of the human soul, Tapan's films hold up a unique mirror to our lives and to the society we live in.

Not many film-makers who succeeded Tapan saw value in his brand of film-making, unfortunately. Through some of his films, he achieved an intangible grace. His body of work echoes across time. His cinema touches you even when it is detached from your own lived reality. That is where it triumphs. No other film-maker in Bengali cinema was so diverse, so commercially successful yet humble like the illustrious Tapan Sinha.

কেন
করলাম ?"
— তপন সিংহ
প্রযোজনা · অরুণ রায়চৌধুরী

# Conclusion

In an interview with the Bengali newspaper, *Sangbad Pratidin*, in July 2002, Tapan lamented, "I don't get any pleasure recollecting any of my films. What I feel are anguish and repentance. When did I do a worthwhile film? Can film ever be a classical art? Even the Hollywood classics of the thirties and forties have been lost. In Indian cinema, artistic and creative excellence can be seen only in a few films. I could find that consistently in the work of only one man—Satyajit Ray. I have made so many films, but I feel now that none of them could fulfil my own expectations. Maybe I couldn't execute what I had in mind. I just feel they could have been much, much better."[1]

Time and again Tapan emphasised that he had made artistic compromises to ensure his films would be commercially viable. Most of his films were indeed enviable box-office successes. According to him, "Everyone needs to compromise. I have compromised keeping the audience in mind. There is not much progress in film appreciation in our country. Film societies have made some impact, but their numbers are insignificant in comparison to the population of Calcutta. I never want my films to be viewed only by the members of film societies. I want them to be watched by a bigger audience. However, if that was the only goal, I could have included fight and dance sequences along with endless songs. But I never did that. When I watched world cinema, I used to be entertained. I had always thought that when I made films, I would provide honest and pure entertainment.

"At times it may not please my aesthetic sensibilities, but if it entertains my audience, I am fine with it. After the release of *Adalat O Ekti Meye*, I got a phone call from a professor at Jadavpur University who told me that since the film was an adult film with an 'A' certificate he didn't take his teenage daughter along with him to watch it. 'But then I felt that she should also watch it and I went to watch it again, this time with her,' he said. That he found something worthy in my film is the kind of communication with my audience I aim to achieve in all my films."[2]

Since the late sixties and the early seventies, when the film society movement was at its peak and the city of Calcutta was shaken by the Naxalite uproar, Tapan's cinema slowly but surely fell out of favour with the 'intellectual' film critics of the city. His films were popular, but he was constantly ignored in discussions on Bengali cinema that bracketed Ray, Sen and Ghatak as its gods. Judged by the aesthetic yardstick calibrated by the European definition of 'good' cinema, Tapan may fall short of these masters on some aspects. However, he developed his own simple, linear narrative style to reveal a deep conscience that has almost always gone down well with the educated film audience. If communicating with a sensitive audience through one's art is one of the objectives of an artist, Tapan definitely makes the cut. To his credit, he worked continuously on his themes, constantly moving from the classical and literary to the naked realities of contemporary urban life. And in doing so, he was far ahead of his time as with his eighties' films like *Adalat O Ekti Meye* and *Atanka*. Few other Bengali directors could depict the crisis of sanity of the middle-class mind to such gripping effect.

In the eighties, Ray, for instance, either made children's films or adapted Tagore's *Ghare Baire* before delving into his most forgettable creation, *Ganashatru* (1989). This film was based on Henrik Ibsen's *An Enemy of the People* in which Dr. Stockmann famously said, 'The strongest man in the world is the man who stands most alone.' It has to be noted that Ray changed the end of his *Ganashatru* to include the role of the 'masses' in an individual's struggle for existence. At about the same time, in his 1991 film, *Ek Doctor Ki Maut*, Tapan, however, restored the Ibsenian touch through Dr. Dipankar Roy who invented a drug to cure leprosy and was constantly harassed by his jealous colleagues. In a claustrophobic society, a genuine talent ends up having to accept defeat in his fight against the petit-bourgeoise middle-class sense of animosity. Dr. Roy has to forego his research temporarily but he finds a new lease of life in his love for his wife. In the end, this belief in the individual and his triumph set Tapan apart from many of his colleagues who had strong Marxist leanings.

In an interview, Tapan once expressed his viewpoint albeit in a different context: "We always say that the people who live in villages are deprived. But in *Sagina Mahato* what the protagonist says is what I find most true—it is impossible to help them by travelling from Calcutta with the romantic notion of revolution. They have to fight their own battle. They have tremendous power within them ... but, what you find in today's literature and films is only the oppression against them. That they have been deprived of their basic rights for centuries is inherent in their folk songs and dances—these are the things to study. Observe the culture of traditional folk instead of thinking about and showing the haplessness of their condition alone."[3] Tapan's frankness understandably did not go down well with the predominant leftist ideology in Bengal's state-level politics and among the Marxist-oriented Bengali middle-class intelligentsia.

In the context of Hindi cinema, Tapan's best parallel could be his friend of the New Theatres days, Hrishikesh Mukherjee. Both of them followed a similar narrative style of simplistic story-telling and directed about 40 feature films each in their careers. In a significant number of their films they spoke about the middle class. Mukherjee's cinema mainly portrayed Bengali life and world view. It just happened that his characters spoke in Hindi. However, conforming to the conventions of commercial Hindi cinema, he had to compromise much more than Tapan in order to make his films more viable for a pan-Indian audience. Aesthetically speaking, Tapan's films were way more superior to Mukherjee's. Keeping Hindi cinema in mind, Tapan's craft can be compared to Bimal Roy's. Roy was Mukherjee's mentor and Tapan's idol when he joined New Theatres. Like Roy's brand of eloquent cinema, Tapan's films of the classical phase, which are based on literary masterpieces, are a treat to watch even today. Roy only made half the number of films that Tapan did. Though he is a much-revered figure in the history of Indian cinema, Roy could not explore as many diverse themes as Tapan since death snatched him away too soon.

To his credit, Tapan took pains to evolve constantly as a film-maker and made films for both adults and children with significant success. Tapan has few equals in the history of Indian cinema. He stands taller than many who are trumpeted as 'legends' by a myopic film-appreciation culture and a biased Hindi-centric national media. His films are watched and rewatched by many even today. Quite a few of them have attained the status of classics.

The music of his films is outstanding. No other director in Bengali cinema apart from Ray has composed music for so many films and with such flair. Siddhartha Kumar Ghosh says: "Tapan could have become a singer if he wanted to … He experimented with songs, background music and a set of instruments. The notes he created were never repetitive … Besides Rabindra Sangeet, his exposure to Indian and Western classical music honed his musical acumen. He was a lifelong student of music. He loved chamber music and his favourite composer was Bach. He appreciated Tchaikovsky, Mussorgsky, Chopin, Beethoven, Mozart and Hayden … After he married Arundhati Devi; his life was filled with aesthetic joy. Music and literature played an important part in their daily life, specifically with reference to Tagore. Arundhati Devi's experience at Santiniketan created the right mindset for the appreciation of art and culture. She contributed to a lifestyle compatible with Sinha's creative pursuits."[4]

Arundhati Devi was born in 1924 at Dhaka, (now in Bangladesh) in the Guha Thakurata family. She grew up in an extraordinarily liberal environment. Her father Bibhucharan Guha Thakurata, who was well versed in Hindu religious texts, also frequented Brahma Samaj meetings, mosques and church assemblies. A gifted singer, Arundhati went to Santiniketan when she was only 12 and her stay there shaped her personality. In a career spanning over two decades, she went on to act in over 30 films. Her last film was Tapan's *Harmonium* (1976). She acted in five of his films including *Jotugriha*, *Jhinder Bandi*, *Kshudhita Pashan* and *Kalamati*. Arundhati also sang in Tapan's *Harmonium* and *Aandhar Periye*. In 1962, *Bhagini Nivedita* (directed by Bijoy Bose), in which Arundhati played the main role, won the President's Gold Medal for the Best Feature Film at the 9th National Film Awards.

In the initial years of their courtship and in their married life, Tagore became a bridge for Tapan and Arundhati to share their common ideals, philosophies and vision. Tapan was one of the few film directors who had read Tagore thoroughly and interpreted the subtle vision of his words onscreen. Tapan and Arundhati would often get together with Santosh Kumar Ghosh, a noted Bengali writer, journalist and an authority on Tagore. Arundhati would sing Tagore songs and Ghosh would explain the background of Tagore's songs, elaborating on their symbolic and metaphorical meanings.

Siddhartha Ghosh reminisces about Arundhati's perfect compatibility with Tapan and her ability to play a complementary role in his life. "She imbibed so many qualities in the world of aesthetics and was admired by many. Paradoxically, as life progressed, she became a practical person and helped Tapan handle many critical issues in life objectively. She relieved him of duties in the mundane world and let him be busy with his own creative pursuits. This motivated Tapan to continue making films even when he became ill and also when he met with an accident during the shooting of *Aaj Ka Robinhood*. Her extraordinary ability to soldier on in difficult times was an eye opener for the entire family. I believe that this extraordinary capacity is reflected in Tapan's film, *Wheel Chair*, which bears a direct relation to Arundhati Devi's experiences."

Arundhati Devi passed away on 16 October 1990 after a prolonged illness. And a double blow came four years later on 19 February when Arundhati's daughter from an earlier marriage (and Tapan's stepdaughter), Anuradha Ghosh, passed away. Ghosh was a connoisseur of Indian classical music and the author of the book, *Ustad Allauddin Khan: The Legend of Music*. Tapan was shattered by her death since the two had shared a close bond. But Tapan was an extremely private man. He seldom discussed his personal life and the pain he had to bear with other people.

At the time of Arundhati Devi's demise, Tapan was working on *Ek Doctor Ki Maut*. He may have drawn on real-life in shaping the sensitively drawn character of Dr. Roy's wife in the film. Equally intriguing was his depiction of the invalid doctor in *Wheel Chair* who fought against medical and physical odds and finally came up triumphant. This film was made at the time when Ghosh was battling cancer. Tapan himself led a very secluded life towards the end—he was confined to bed due to illness. This was extremely distressing for an individual who was fond of adventure and whose films had made extensive use of outdoor locations. Suffering from pneumonia, he passed away on 15 January 2009.

In 2006, the National Film Awards committee conferred the prestigious Dadasaheb Phalke Award (the highest award in Indian cinema) on Tapan. Siddhartha Kumar Ghosh laments: "When the committee took the decision to award him, it was too late. He was so seriously ill that he could not go to Delhi to receive it ... Thanks are due to Mr. Priya Ranjan Dasmunshi who instituted an award—to mark sixty years of Indian Independence—for individuals who contributed to excellence in different fields of art. He and the then Governor of West Bengal came to felicitate Tapan at his residence. Tapan was seriously ill. I was there to witness the historic occasion, which was telecast on television. This was a tribute to a person who not only created good films for a generation to admire but also helped the film industry to survive many challenges across five decades and sustain several technicians who worked in it. Tapan viewed film-making as an industry and believed that subjective experimentation at the cost of the financier was meaningless. That is why most of his films while receiving creative recognition also made producers happy."

It is unfortunate that cine-scholars and academics have shown very little interest in Tapan's body of work. Sanjay Mukherjee, former Head of the Department of Film Studies, Jadavpur University, regrets the absence of writing on Tapan Sinha by film society magazines in general. "Most of the discussions and writings by film societies in the fifties and sixties revolved around Satyajit Ray. So, the likes of Tapan Sinha, Barin Saha and Ajoy Kar were never discussed at all. The so-called intellectuals of that time suffered from a complex that our cinema wasn't worthwhile when compared to that of the West. Ray's cinema was appreciated in Europe right from the beginning, and the perception gained ground that films that were not similar to Ray's must not be that good. On top of this, Tapan Sinha decried Marxist ideology in his films, sometimes openly as in *Sagina Mahato* or in a subtle way as in *Galpa Holeo Satyi*."

Mukherjee's colleague at Jadavpur University, Moinak Biswas, holds similar views about why Tapan Sinha was neglected in discussions on serious cinema. "At that time, the division of "art" vs "commercial" cinema was in vogue. Tapan Sinha had always been vocal about his debt to Hollywood, which was the biggest devil for the film societies in a sense. Tapan Sinha along with the likes of Ajoy Kar and Tarun Majumder were making films which can be termed 'quasi-commercial'. And they did compromise a bit, I think. This is why they were never discussed at that time. Only in the late eighties, when the subjects and themes of film society magazines became varied, the likes of Tapan Sinha gained prominence in them. There were special issues on him then, probably because film societies started realising their mistake in ignoring him for so long." Veteran film scholar Shamik Bandopadhyay puts the stance taken by the critics associated with film societies during the fifties and sixties in context. "Bohurupee staged their play *Raktakarabi* (Red Flower) in 1954 and *Pather Panchali* by Satyajit Ray was released in 1955. These two events were major influences on my generation. In parallel, the real impact of Jibanananda Das (who died in 1954), one of the greatest Bengali poets, was being felt as well. To us, any play or film which had even a slightest semblance of a commercial venture was an outcast at that time. Soon, Ritwik Ghatak and Mrinal Sen also emerged for us along with Ray, and Tapan Sinha's cinema was forgotten.

"We got involved with the Calcutta Film Society and started watching international classics of Ingmar Bergman, Akira Kurosawa and Michelangelo Antonioni. We believed we had a responsibility to this type of cinema because it was rare. We became partisans and tried to fight a battle for the type of cinema we loved. In the process, not deliberately but unconsciously, we ignored Tapan Sinha's cinema. It was not about him alone, we did distinguish between the cinema of Satyajit, Ritwik Ghatak and Mrinal Sen too."

It is quite unfortunate that while analysing film as an art form gained prominence in the fifties, cinema that deliberately wanted to tread a different path was neglected. Tapan Sinha and a few other Bengali directors became a victim of this neglect. Some of them faded away, unable to cope with rejection from the elite, educated class they themselves belonged to. To Tapan's credit, he hung on and continued to make films that would reap dividends at the box office as well be artistic and thoughtful. This enabled him to experiment with his themes, cast and genres. In the end, he made his point by having most film societies publish special issues on his cinema. Most importantly, he remained a shelter for the middle-class, educated Bengali, a part of their mundane existence, a reflection of their inconsequence. The cinema of Bengal's triumvirate had always instilled respect and pride, but Tapan's films were the ones in which generations of Bengalis lived in during the five glorious decades of his film-making.

***

A number of Tapan's films have been lost or damaged completely over the years and many of the surviving ones are not in a watchable condition. His *Ankush, Tonsil* and *Kalamati* are not available anymore. Tragically, apart from Ray's films, very few works by Bengali film-makers have been digitally restored. A Tapan Sinha Foundation exists, but insufficient resources have hampered its efforts at reviving interest in his cinema. The Foundation needs to urgently address the archiving aspect of Tapan's cinema and it deserves all the help it can get.

Like many a typical educated Bengali of the last century, Tapan was an impeccable gentleman who refrained from blowing his own trumpet. Rather, he always questioned his art and tried to undermine it himself. If Tapan were around today, would he get more recognition than he received during his time? There is not an iota of doubt that he deserved more. He chose to remain humble, reclusive and impeccably restrained—traits of a bygone era. It was his misfortune that he and his work were constantly compared with the cinema and the cultural positioning of Satyajit Ray. Despite such comparisons, Tapan chose to remain grounded, a man happy to live in his own world. But he opened up the whole world to us in his films.

## REFERENCES

[1] Tapan Sinha, *Chalachchitra Ajibon*, Ed: Shamik Bandopadhyay, Dey's Publishing, 2009, p. 366 [Translation by the author]

[2] Nandan Mitra, *Tapan Sinha-r Film-making*, Chalachitra o Sanskriti Charcha Kendra, January 2015, p. 25

[3] Ibid., p. 18

[4] Siddhartha Kumar Ghosh, 'A Film-maker Extraordinary', Tapan Sinha: A Tribute, *Cine Central*, 2 October 2009, p. 50

# Awards

| Award | Year | Film | Recipient |
|---|---|---|---|
| National Film Award for Best Feature Film in Bengali | 1956 | Kabuliwala | |
| National Film Award for Best Feature Film | 1956 | Kabuliwala | |
| Berlin Film Festival Silver Bear Extraordinary Prize of the Jury for Music | 1956 | Kabuliwala | Ravi Shankar |
| Certificate of Merit for Second Best Feature Film in Bengali | 1957 | Louhakapat | |
| All India Certificate of Merit for Second Best Feature Film | 1960 | Kshudhita Pashan | |
| Award at the Ireland Cork Film Festival | 1960 | Kshudhita Pashan | |
| Certificate of Merit for Third Best Feature Film | 1964 | Jotugriha | |
| Best Actress Award at the International Film Festival of India | 1963 | Nirjan Saikate | Chhaya Devi, Renuka Roy, Bharati Devi, Ruma Guha Thakurta, Sharmila Tagore |
| President's Silver Medal for Best Feature Film in Bengali | 1964 | Arohi | |

| | | | |
|---|---|---|---|
| All India Certificate of Merit for Best Story Writer | 1964 | Arohi | Banaphool |
| Locarno Film Festival Interfilm Award | 1965 | Arohi | |
| London Film Festival Certificate of Merit | 1965 | Arohi | |
| All India Certificate of Merit for Second Best Feature Film | 1965 | Atithi | |
| Venice Film Festival Certificate of Merit | 1965 | Atithi | |
| National Film Award for Best Feature Film in Bengali | 1966 | Galpa Holeo Satyi | |
| National Film Award for Best Feature Film | 1967 | Hatey Bazarey | |
| Locarno Film Festival Silver Trophy | 1967 | Hatey Bazarey | |
| Phnom Penh Asian Film Festival (Cambodia) Best Film (Silver Cup) | 1968 | Hatey Bazarey | |
| National Film Award for Best Feature Film in Bengali | 1968 | Aponjon | |
| National Film Award for Best Screenplay | 1971 | Ekhoni | |
| Moscow Film Festival Afro-Asian Award | 1971 | Sagina Mahato | |
| National Film Award for Best Music Direction | 1972 | Zindagi Zindagi | Sachin Dev Burman |
| Asian Film Festival, Seoul, South Korea Award for Music | 1976 | Harmonium | |
| Asian Film Festival, Seoul, South Korea Golden Crown for Best Actress | 1976 | Harmonium | Sonali Gupta |
| National Film Award for Best Feature Film in Bengali | 1976 | Ek Je Chhilo Desh | |
| National Film Award for Best Children's Film | 1977 | Safed Haathi | |

| National Film Award for Best Feature Film in Bengali | 1981 | Adalat O Ekti Meye | |
|---|---|---|---|
| Nargis Dutt Award for Best Feature Film on National Integration | 1984 | Aadmi Aur Aurat | |
| Berlin Film Festival Unicef Award—Honourable Mention | 1988 | Aaj Ka Robinhood | |
| National Film Award for Best Direction | 1990 | Ek Doctor Ki Maut | |
| National Film Award for Second Best Feature Film | 1990 | Ek Doctor Ki Maut | |
| Special Jury Award (Acting) | 1990 | Ek Doctor Ki Maut | Pankaj Kapur |
| National Film Award for Best Feature Film in Bengali | 1991 | Antardhan | |
| Special Jury Award (Acting) | 1991 | Antardhan | Soumitra Chatterjee |
| National Film Award for Best Film on Other Social Issues | 1994 | Wheel Chair | |

Source: *Tapan Sinha Special Issue–Chitravas*, Vol. 38 (No. 1 to 4), January–December 2003, pp. 108–114

## Notable Honours

Honorary Key to the city of San Francisco conferred by the Mayor–1962
Padma Shri from the Government of India–1992
Honorary D.Litt. from Rabindra Bharati University–1997
Deshikottam, Honorary D.Litt. from Visva-Bharati University–1999
Citizen's Felicitation, Calcutta Municipality Corporation–1999
Satyajit Ray Award, Haldia Utsav–2004
Dadasaheb Phalke Award for Lifetime Achievement–2006

# Filmography

## Feature Films

**1954 |** *Ankush*, B/W, Bengali

Story: Narayan Ganguly | Script: Tapan Sinha, Bolin Shome

Cinematography: Anil Bandopadhyay | Editing: Rabi Sen

Music: Kalipada Sen | Producer: Little Pictures

Cast: Anubha Gupta, Manju Dey, Abhi Bhattacharjee, Shyam Laha and others

**1955 |** *Upahar*, B/W, Bengali

Story: Sailajananda Mukhopadhyay | Script: Tapan Sinha

Cinematography: Anil Bandopadhyay | Editing: Subodh Roy

Music: Kalipada Sen | Producer: Bani Chitram

Cast: Kanu Bandopadhyay, Uttam Kumar, Nirmal Kumar, Manju Dey, Sabitri Chatterjee and others

**1956 |** *Tonsil*, B/W, Bengali

Story: Bibhutibhusan Mukhopadhyay | Script: Tapan Sinha

Cinematography: Anil Bandopadhyay | Editing: Subodh Roy

Music: Shailesh Roy | Producer: Bani Chitram

Cast: Kali Bandopadhyay, Satya Bandopadhyay, Bhanu Bandopadhyay, Jahar Roy, Madhuri (Madhabi) Mukhopadhyay and others

**1957 |** *Kabuliwala*, B/W, Bengali

Story: Rabindranath Tagore | Script: Tapan Sinha

Cinematography: Anil Bandopadhyay | Editing: Subodh Roy

Music: Ravi Shankar | Producer: Charuchitra

Cast: Chhabi Biswas, Tinku Thakur, Manju Dey, Radhamohan Bhattacharjee and others

**1958**

*Louhakapat*, B/W, Bengali

Story: Jarasandha | Script: Tapan Sinha

Cinematography: Bimal Mukhopadhyay | Editing: Subodh Roy

Music: Pankaj Mullick | Producer: L.B. Films International

Cast: Chhabi Biswas, Kali Bandopadhyay, Nirmal Kumar, Mala Sinha, Manju Dey and others

*Kalamati*, B/W, Bengali

Story: Ramapada Chaudhuri | Script: Piyush Basu

Cinematography: Anil Bandopadhyay | Editing: Subodh Roy

Music: Ravi Shankar | Producer: Tash Films

Cast: Asit Baran, Arundhati Devi, Anil Chatterjee and others

**1959 |** *Khaniker Atithi*, B/W, Bengali

Story: Nirmal Kumar Sengupta | Script: Tapan Sinha

Cinematography: Anil Bandopadhyay | Editing: Subodh Roy

Music: Hemanta Mukhopadhyay | Producer: S.B. Films Private Limited

Cast: Nirmal Kumar, Ruma Guha Thakurta, Chhabi Biswas, Radhamohan Bhattacharjee and others

**1960 |** *Kshudhita Pashan*, B/W, Bengali

Story: Rabindranath Tagore | Script: Tapan Sinha

Cinematography: Bimal Mukhopadhyay | Editing: Subodh Roy

Music: Ali Akbar Khan | Producer: Eastern Circuit Private Limited

Cast: Arundhati Devi, Soumitra Chatterjee, Chhabi Biswas, Radhamohan Bhattacharjee and others

**1961 |** *Jhinder Bandi*, B/W, Bengali

Story: Saradindu Bandopadhyay | Script: Tapan Sinha

Cinematography: Bimal Mukhopadhyay | Editing: Subodh Roy

Music: Ali Akbar Khan | Producer: B.N. Roy Productions

Cast: Uttam Kumar, Arundhati Devi, Soumitra Chatterjee, Radhamohan Bhattacharjee and others

**1962 |** *Hanshuli Banker Upakatha*, B/W, Bengali

Story: Tarashankar Bandopadhyay | Script: Tapan Sinha

Cinematography: Bimal Mukhopadhyay | Editing: Subodh Roy

Music: Hemanta Mukhopadhyay | Producer: Jalan Productions

Cast: Kali Bandopadhyay, Rabi Ghosh, Dilip Roy, Anubha Gupta and others

**1963 |** *Nirjan Saikate,* B/W, Bengali

Story: Kalkut (Samaresh Basu) | Script: Tapan Sinha

Cinematography: Bimal Mukhopadhyay | Editing: Subodh Roy

Music: Kalipada Sen | Producer: New Theatres (Exhibitors) Private Limited

Cast: Chhaya Devi, Bharati Devi, Renuka Devi, Ruma Guha Thakurata, Sharmila Tagore, Anil Chatterjee and others

**1964**

*Jotugriha,* B/W, Bengali

Story: Subodh Ghosh | Script: Tapan Sinha

Cinematography: Bimal Mukhopadhyay | Editing: Subodh Roy

Music: Asish Khan | Producer: Uttam Kumar Films Private Limited

Cast: Uttam Kumar, Arundhati Devi, Anil Chatterjee and others

*Arohi,* B/W, Bengali

Story: Banaphool | Script: Tapan Sinha

Cinematography: Bimal Mukhopadhyay | Editing: Subodh Roy

Music: Hemanta Mukhopadhyay | Producer: Ashim Pal Productions

Cast: Kali Bandopadhyay, Bikash Roy, Chhaya Devi, Rabi Ghosh and others

**1965 |** *Atithi,* B/W, Bengali

Story: Rabindranath Tagore | Script: Tapan Sinha

Cinematography: Dilipranjan Mukhopadhyay | Editing: Subodh Roy

Music: Tapan Sinha | Producer: New Theatres (Exhibitors) Private Limited

Cast: Partho Mukhopadhyay, Basabi Bannerjee, Ajitesh Bandopadhyay and others

**1966 |** *Galpa Holeo Satyi,* B/W, Bengali

Story: Tapan Sinha | Script: Tapan Sinha

Cinematography: Bimal Mukhopadhyay | Editing: Subodh Roy

Music: Tapan Sinha | Producer: New Theatres (Exhibitors) Private Limited

Cast: Rabi Ghosh, Chhaya Devi, Bharati Devi, Bhanu Bandopadhyay and others

**1967 |** *Hatey Bazarey,* B/W, Bengali

Story: Banaphool | Script: Tapan Sinha

Cinematography: Dinen Gupta | Editing: Subodh Roy

Music: Tapan Sinha | Producer: Priya Films

Cast: Ashok Kumar, Vyjayanthimala, Chhaya Devi, Ajitesh Bandopadhyay, Chinmoy Roy and others

**1968 |** *Aponjon,* B/W, Bengali

Story: Indramitra | Script: Tapan Sinha

Cinematography: Bimal Mukhopadhyay | Editing: Subodh Roy

Music: Tapan Sinha | Producer: K.L. Kapoor Productions

Cast: Chhaya Devi, Samit Bhanja, Swarup Dutta, Sumita Sanyal, Nirmal Kumar and others

**1970**

*Sagina Mahato,* B/W, Bengali

Story: Rupodorshi (Gourkishore Ghosh) | Script: Tapan Sinha

Cinematography: Bimal Mukhopadhyay | Editing: Subodh Roy

Music: Tapan Sinha | Producer: Rupashree International

Cast: Dilip Kumar, Saira Bano, Anil Chatterjee, Swarup Dutta, Sumita Sanyal and others

*Sagina*, Colour, Hindi (remake of *Sagina Mahato*)

Story: Rupodorshi (Gourkishore Ghosh) | Script: K Abbas

Cinematography: Bimal Mukhopadhyay | Editing: Subodh Roy

Music: Sachin Dev Burman | Producer: Rupashree International

Cast: Dilip Kumar, Saira Bano, Anil Chatterjee, Swarup Dutta, Aparna Sen and others

**1971 |** *Ekhoni*, B/W, Bengali

Story: Ramapada Chaudhuri | Script: Tapan Sinha

Cinematography: Bimal Mukhopadhyay | Editing: Subodh Roy

Music: Tapan Sinha | Producer: K.L. Kapoor Productions

Cast: Aparna Sen, Swarup Dutta, Nirmal Kumar, Mousumi Chatterjee and others

**1972 |** *Zindagi Zindagi*, Colour, Hindi (remake of *Khaniker Atithi*)

Story: Tapan Sinha | Script: K.A. Abbas

Cinematography: Nariman Irani | Editing: Subodh Roy

Music: Sachin Dev Burman | Producer: Nariman Irani

Cast: Waheeda Rehman, Sunil Dutt, Ashok Kumar and others

**1973 | *Aandhar Periye*,** B/W (partly colour), Bengali

Story: Chittaranjan Maiti | Script: Tapan Sinha

Cinematography: Bimal Mukhopadhyay | Editing: Subodh Roy

Music: Tapan Sinha | Producer: Satyasudha Productions

Cast: Madhabi Mukhopadhyay, Subhendu Chatterjee, Nirmal Kumar, Sumitra Mukhopadhyay and others

**1975 | *Raja*,** B/W, Bengali

Story: Prafulla Roy | Script: Tapan Sinha

Cinematography: Bimal Mukhopadhyay | Editing: Subodh Roy

Music: Tapan Sinha | Producer: A.R.C. Productions

Cast: Debraj Roy, Samit Bhanja, Nirmal Kumar, Arati Bhattacharjee, Mahua Roychoudhury and others

**1976 | *Harmonium*,** B/W, Bengali

Story: Tapan Sinha | Script: Tapan Sinha

Cinematography: Bimal Mukhopadhyay | Editing: Subodh Roy

Music: Tapan Sinha | Producer: Nilkamal Movies

Cast: Arundhati Devi, Chhaya Devi, Samit Bhanja, Swarup Dutta, Anil Chatterjee and others

**1977 | *Ek Je Chhilo Desh*,** B/W, Bengali

Story: Shankar | Script: Tapan Sinha

Cinematography: Bimal Mukhopadhyay | Editing: Subodh Roy

Music: Tapan Sinha | Producer: K.L. Kapoor Films

Cast: Dipankar Dey, Chhaya Devi, Kali Bandopadhyay, Rabi Ghosh, Anil Chatterjee and others

**1978 |** *Safed Haathi*, Colour, Hindi

Story: Tapan Sinha | Script: Tapan Sinha

Cinematography: Bimal Mukhopadhyay | Editing: Subodh Roy

Music: Ravindra Jain | Producer: R.A. Jalan

Cast: Shatrughan Sinha, Vijay Arora, Sadhu Meher, Aswini Agarwal and others

**1979 |** *Sabuj Dwiper Raja*, Colour, Bengali

Story: Sunil Ganguly | Script: Tapan Sinha

Cinematography: Bimal Mukhopadhyay | Editing: Subodh Roy

Music: Tapan Sinha | Producer: Children's Film Society of India

Cast: Samit Bhanja, Nirmal Kumar, Biplab Chatterjee, Kalyan Chatterjee and others

**1980 |** *Banchharamer Bagan*, Colour, Bengali

Story: Manoj Mitra | Script: Tapan Sinha

Cinematography: Bimal Mukhopadhyay | Editing: Subodh Roy

Music: Tapan Sinha | Producer: D.K. Films Enterprise

Cast: Manoj Mitra, Dipankar Dey, Madhabi Mukhopadhyay, Nirmal Kumar, Biplab Chatterjee and others

**1982 |** *Adalat O Ekti Meye*, Colour, Bengali

Story: Tapan Sinha | Script: Tapan Sinha

Cinematography: Bimal Mukhopadhyay | Editing: Subodh Roy

Music: Tapan Sinha | Producer: D.K. Films Enterprise

Cast: Tanuja, Manoj Mitra, Nirmal Kumar, Debika Mukhopadhyay and others

**1985 |** *Baidurya Rahasya*, Colour, Bengali
Story: Tapan Sinha | Script: Tapan Sinha
Cinematography: Bimal Mukhopadhyay | Editing: Subodh Roy
Music: Tapan Sinha | Producer: Saraswati Chitram
Cast: Basanta Chowdhury, Alpana Goswami, Moonmoon Sen, Tapas Pal, Manoj Mitra and others

**1986 |** *Atanka*, Colour, Bengali
Story: Tapan Sinha | Script: Tapan Sinha
Cinematography: Kamal Nayek | Editing: Subodh Roy
Music: Tapan Sinha | Producer: Charuchitra
Cast: Soumitra Chatterjee, Satabi Roy, Prosenjit, Sumanta Mukhopadhyay and others

**1987 |** *Aaj Ka Robinhood*, Colour, Hindi
Story: Tapan Sinha | Script: Tapan Sinha
Cinematography: Kamal Nayek | Editing: Subodh Roy
Music: Tapan Sinha | Producer: R.A. Jalan
Cast: Ritesh Talwar, Anil Chatterjee, Utpal Dutt, Rabi Ghosh and others

**1991 |** *Ek Doctor Ki Maut*, Colour, Hindi
Story: Ramapada Chaudhuri | Script: Tapan Sinha
Cinematography: Soumendu Roy | Editing: Subodh Roy
Music: Tapan Sinha | Producer: NFDC
Cast: Pankaj Kapur, Shabana Azmi, Deepa Sahi, Vijayendra, Basanta Chowdhury and others

**1992 |** *Antardhan*, Colour, Bengali
Story: Dibyendu Palit | Script: Tapan Sinha
Cinematography: Soumendu Roy | Editing: Subodh Roy

Music: Tapan Sinha | Producer: Naba Chanda and Swapan Mitra

Cast: Soumitra Chatterjee, Madhabi Mukhopadhyay, Satabi Roy, Arjun Chakraborty and others

**1994 |** *Wheel Chair*, Colour, Bengali

Story: Tapan Sinha | Script: Tapan Sinha

Cinematography: Soumendu Roy | Editing: Subodh Roy

Music: Tapan Sinha | Producer: NFDC

Cast: Soumitra Chatterjee, Laboni Sarkar, Arjun Chakraborty, Manoj Mitra and others

**1998 |** *Ajab Gayer Ajab Katha*, Colour, Bengali

Story: Sirshendu Mukhopadhyay | Script: Tapan Sinha

Cinematography: Soumendu Roy | Editing: Snehasis Ganguly

Music: Tapan Sinha | Producer: Venkatesh Films

Cast: Soumitra Chatterjee, Debesh Roychowdhury, Nirmal Kumar and others

**2000 |** *Anokha Moti*, Colour, Hindi

Story: Tapan Sinha | Script: Tapan Sinha

Cinematography: Soumendu Roy | Editing: Snehasis Ganguly

Music: Tapan Sinha | Producer: Gouranga Films

Cast: Arjun Chakraborty, Nayab Aftab and others

**Short Films**

**1982 |** *Aadmi Aur Aurat*, Colour, Hindi, Telefilm

Story: Prafulla Roy | Script: Tapan Sinha

Cinematography: Kamal Nayek | Editing: Subodh Roy
Music: Tapan Sinha | Producer: Doordarshan
Cast: Amol Palekar, Mahua Roychoudhury and others

**1983 |** *Manush*, Colour, Bengali, Telefilm
Story: Prafulla Roy | Script: Tapan Sinha
Cinematography: Kamal Nayek | Editing: Subodh Roy
Music: Tapan Sinha | Producer: Films Division
Cast: Samit Bhanja, Debika Mukhopadhyay and others

**1989 |** *Didi*, Colour, Hindi, Telefilm
Story: Premendra Mitra | Script: Tapan Sinha
Cinematography: Kamal Nayek | Editing: Subodh Roy
Music: Tapan Sinha | Producer: Doordarshan
Cast: Deepti Naval, Vivek Talwar, Bhisma Guha Thakurata and others

**1996 |** *Satabdir Kanya*, Colour, Hindi, five short films
Script: Tapan Sinha | Cinematography: Soumendu Roy
Editing: Subodh Roy, Snehasis Ganguly | Music: Tapan Sinha | Producer: Sunya Media

*Kadambini* **|** Story: Rabindranath Tagore
Cast: Shabana Azmi, Papiya Sen and others

*Abhagi* | Story: Sarat Chandra Chattopadhyay
Cast: Jaya Bachchan, Arjun Chakraborty, Joy Badlani and others

*Champia* | Story: Prafulla Roy
Cast: Deepa Sahi, Jnanesh Mukhopadhyay and others

*Charu* | Story: Gourkishore Ghosh
Cast: Nandita Das, Milind Gunaji, Debasree Roy and others

*Hemlata* | Story: Dibyendyu Palit
Cast: Sulabha Deshpande, Debasree Roy, Koushik Sen, Arjun Chakraborty and others

**1997** | *Hutomer Naksha*, Colour, Bengali, 13-episode Televison Serial (Doordarshan)
Story: Tapan Sinha | Script: Tapan Sinha
Cinematography: Soumendu Roy | Editing: Subrata Roy
Music: Tapan Sinha | Producer: Ramlal Nandi
Cast: Soumitra Chatterjee, Rabi Ghosh, Nirmal Kumar, Rita Koiral, Manoj Mitra and others

**2005** | *Char Charitra*, Colour, Bengali, Telefilm
Story: Tapan Sinha | Script: Tapan Sinha
Cinematography: Soumik Haldar | Editing: Subhrabaran Mitra
Music: Dilip Roy | Producer: E-TV Bangla
Cast: Soumitra Chatterjee, Madhabi Mukhopadhyay and others

**Documentary Films**

**1959** | *Jagadish Chandra Bose*
Script: Tapan Sinha
Cinematography: Gopal Sanyal, David Holmes | Editing: Subodh Roy
Music: Shailesh Roy | Producer: Tapan Sinha and Films Division

(The title card of the documentary has Pijush Bose's name as director though he was ably and amply guided and supported by Tapan Sinha while making this film.)

**1962 |** *Aamar Desh*

Filmed during the war between India and China, the documentary starred Uttam Kumar, Suchitra Sen, Sandhya Roy, Bikash Roy and others.

**1994 |** *Ajana Shatru* (on AIDS)

Story: Tapan Sinha | Script: Tapan Sinha
Cinematography: Soumendu Roy | Editing: Subodh Roy
Cast: Soumitra Chatterjee, Manoj Mitra and others

# Acknowledgements

Writing a biography of Tapan Sinha was a tall order for me. Like any Bengali born before 1980 in Calcutta, I was fortunate to be brought up in an environment that fostered culture—literary and cinematic. We could go and watch the films of the master film-makers of Bengal. Blind copies of Hindi and south-Indian films were not lapping at the shores of the Bay of Bengal then. Tapan's films were a regular part of our cinematic meal—his children's films first, then, as we grew up, his black-and-white classics and contemporary colour films. Tapan was a beloved director of many while I was growing up. Yet, writing a book on him and his cinema was a difficult task.

This was primarily because I had very few sources to gather information from. Tapan's three short memoirs are collected in an important volume called *Chalachchitra Ajiban*, published by Dey's Publishing in 2009, the year of his death. The collection of interviews on Tapan Sinha, edited by Nandan Mitra, was another source. Other available books and magazine retrospectives including the ones by Cine Central and Chitravas, focused on Tapan's cinema rather than his persona.

I am hugely indebted to my friend Sounak Chacraverti for giving me the first flicker of an idea to write a book on Tapan.

Many thanks to Siddhartha Kumar Ghosh who gave me rare insights into the legend's mind and helped me to understand the progression of Tapan's cinematic journey. He also took the time to read the entire manuscript and point out the factual irregularities in an earlier draft. I am also indebted to Anindya Sinha for putting me in touch with the right people and answering my questions. He has also generously shared a number of pictures.

Thanks to Sounak Gupta for sharing the covers of film booklets and to my dear friend Shoma A. Chatterji for giving me access to several pictures in her collection. I am thankful to Amol Palekar, Deepti Naval, Goutam Ghose, Madhabi Mukhopadhyay, Nandita Das, Pankaj Kapur, Purnima Dutta, Shabana Azmi and Sharmila Tagore for their valuable inputs on working with Tapan Sinha. I am also indebted to film scholars Moinak Biswas, Sajal Datta, Shamik Bandopadhyay and Sanjay Mukherjee for providing information on Tapan's acceptance or rather the lack of it, among film society members.

As was the case with my previous books on cinema, the films of the subject of this book haunted me for months. I realised the beauty of Tapan's cinematic traits—his tracking shots, persistent use of long shots and rare portraitures. My painter and writer friend Shiladitya Sarkar, as always, helped me with some great conversations on Tapan's cinema, particularly about the use of landscape and music.

Abesh Kumar Das's analytic book, *Tapan Sinha: Sarbik Chalachchitra Biksha* (Sristisukh Prokashan LLP, 2016), was a great help to me. I had the good fortune of discussing the subject with Das at length. Those discussions helped me to take an in-depth look at Tapan's work and reassess him as a master film-maker. Das also shared many pictures of Tapan with me.

I am thankful to the photographer Sukumar Roy, who provided me with pictures from his eclectic collection. It is a shame he passed away before this book could see the light of day.

I am also indebted to Soumitra Chatterjee who shared many valuable insights on Tapan with me. Not everything is to be written about, but the anecdotes were a great help in letting me connect the dots.